# Transfer of Training in Sports

Volume III

By

Dr. Anatoliy P. Bondarchuk

Translated from Russian by
Jake Jensen

Edited by
Matt Thome MS, CSCS
J. Bryan Mann, Ph.D

Transfer of Training in Sports

# Volume III

## By
## Dr. Anatoliy P. Bondarchuk

Translated by Jake Jensen

Edited by
Matt Thome MS, CSCS
J. Bryan Mann, Ph.D

Published by:
Ultimate Athlete Concepts
Michigan, USA
2017
For information or to order copies: www.uaconcepts.com

Bondarchuk, Anatoliy P.

Critique of the Soviet Methods / Anatoliy P. Bondarchuk

Includes Bibliographical References.

ISBN – 13: 978-1981828203

ISBN – 10: 1981828206

Printed in the United States of America

Ultimate Athlete Concepts
Website: www.uaconcepts.com

# Table of Contents

# About the Author

## Dr. Anatoliy P. Bondarchuk

Dr. Anatoliy P. Bondarchuk is renowned as an athlete (1972 Olympic Champion and European Champion in the hammer throw as well as a former World Record holder) and Dr. Bondarchuk's coaching credentials are virtually unprecedented in sport.

Dr. Bondarchuk is a Doctor of Pedagogical Science (University of Kyiv) and his research into technique and high-performance training methods formed the basis for many of the common techniques and practices used by the world's top athletes today. Dr. Bondarchuk developed the USSR National Team throws program from 1976 to 1992 from which he produced numerous World and Olympic Champions in the Hammer, Discus, and Shot Put. He has authored 11 books and 195 articles in his areas of expertise. A common focus is training to maintain performance and technique. Since 1992 he has coached for Portugal and Kuwait.

Dr. Bondarchuk's athletes, while members of the USSR National Team, broke 12 World Records and still hold the current world record in the hammer throw. His athletes won all hammer throw medals in 4 consecutive, non-boycotted Olympic Games.

# Foreword

My dearest readers, in this book you will find the logical progression of the *Transfer of Training in Sports* series. This series has historically addressed the nuances and systems of developing transfer of training in speed-strength sports. *Transfer of Training in Sports* has systematically examined fact-based material, poured over decades of research, and built the case for the Bondarchuk system of training in athletes of all qualifications from beginners to perennial Olympic Champions. Many years have passed since the research used in this series was completed and published. In my view, it only makes sense that the system of training athletes in our time reflects the advances made. This means the system of training today should differ from that which was used in the 1970's to the 1990's, prior to the monumental advances made in these years. In order to examine these conformational changes (if they indeed occurred), we must revisit all of the athletes of various training qualifications who were trained since the 2000's and question them. This questionnaire must be focused on the specific test indicators that were examined in the 70's and 80's. In addition, we must set threshold indicators demonstrated by athletes in the strength, jump, and running disciplines (speed-strength disciplines) of track and field, across all of the various levels of sports mastery. In my opinion, these can help expose the issue of transfer of training from the paradigm of the critical nature of using test exercises in preparing athletes. This is especially true when examining specific indicators of fitness and sports performance. In other words, setting an optimal threshold (for example, in strength indicators), being careful not to set it too high, in order to achieve the corresponding result in competition exercises.

The second problem is twofold and relates to the aforementioned intent of transfer of training. First, in the theory and practice of physical preparation, we see that transfer is a process of transferring sports form from one exercise to another. In addition, we must examine the process of transfer of training in speed-strength disciplines of track and field from the perspective of the interaction between the fast and slow twitch muscle fibers. What I mean specifically, is the interplay between the two types of muscle fibers in the process of completing both slow and fast movements through the spectrum of general to specific exercises. In my view, having a correlation will change our outlook of the process of transfer of training (in speed-strength events, specifically) to a much more significant degree than any other factor. This means, first and foremost, that achieving the aforementioned threshold for physical preparation in one or another accessory exercise is critical.

Finally, examining the transfer of training in types of endurance, from the point of view of existing examples of the bioenergetics of muscle actions in aerobic, glycolytic, and phosphagen exercises.

I would like to express my deepest gratitude for each and every one of the coaches, athletes, and also the contributors from the various Federations of the Soviet Socialist Republic who helped in the monumental task of compiling and examining the experimental material for this work over the course of more than a decade.  Thank you.

# Chapter 1: Transfer of Training in Sprint Disciplines

In this chapter we will discuss the results of experimental data (a cross examination of coaches and athletes of various sport qualification) that were compiled during the years between 2000 and 2015. This data has been compared to similar numbers obtained for the years from 1980 – 2000. Initially I would have assumed that the results that were obtained concerning the transfer of training in last 15 years would differ from those that were obtained from 1980 to 2000. I made this assumption for one main reason: the systems for preparing athletes *must* have improved in the last 15 years, compared to the advances made in the 20 years prior to the year 2000. What is more, I reason that most track and field events *must* have made huge jumps in world records and overall top performances as compared to those from 1980-2000.

In keeping with the goal of comparing the systematic transfer of training over the course of the aforementioned periods of time, we will look at experimental tests using the exact same test indicators. In addition, transfer between them will be cross-examined using correlational analysis. This means that the greater the coefficient value, the more closely correlated the two test indicators are. In running these correlational analyses, the lowest correlational number was 0.380.

Table 1.1 shows the results of correlational analysis for indicators of preparation in male 100m sprinters between competition and special-preparatory exercises. They demonstrate the presence of a high level of correlation between the two. In most cases, the correlation coefficient is located in the range of 0.700 - 0.800. The highest coefficient (0.888) was between sprints of 150m and 200m and the lowest (0.700) was tied between sprints of 30m and the 200m dash. 60m sprints were also comparable to the 200m dash; both were equally correlated at 0.700. If we compare these values of correlational coefficients with their analogous numbers in the preceding decade, we see that they do not differ much, if at all. In the analysis done in more recent years, there were 8 cases where the correlation rose above 0.800; the same is true for the period of 1980 – 2000. A slight difference is observed in the lower correlational results, however. Here we see that the lowest correlation in the earlier data was 0.607, and the more recent analysis shows a lowest correlation of 0.700.

Table 1.1 – Indicators of correlational relationships for male 100m sprinters in several running exercises.

| Number | | 1 | 2 | 3 | 4 | 5 | 6 | 7 |
|---|---|---|---|---|---|---|---|---|
| | Exer. | 30m sprint stand. start | 30m sprint from blocks | 60m sprint from blocks | 100m sprint from blocks | 120m sprint from blocks | 150m sprint from blocks | 200m sprint from blocks |
| 1 | 30m sprint stand. start | - | 0.712 0.755 | 0.707 0.834 | 0.780 0.778 | 0.765 0.797 | 0.778 0.768 | 0.724 0.715 |
| 2 | 30m sprint from blocks | | - | 0.844 0.803 | 0.837 0.866 | 0.798 0.796 | 0.805 0.777 | 0.780 0.712 |
| 3 | 60m sprint from blocks | | | - | 0.764 0.788 | 0.757 0.807 | 0.773 0.756 | 0.750 0.705 |
| 4 | 100m sprint from blocks | | | | - | 0.741 0.798 | 0.773 0.779 | 0.834 0.764 |
| 5 | 120m sprint from blocks | | | | | - | 0.765 0.798 | 0.780 0.761 |
| 6 | 150m sprint from blocks | | | | | | - | 0.888 0.853 |
| 7 | 200m sprint from blocks | | | | | | | - |

**** Author's Note ****
Here and throughout this book the numerator in each box is the indicator for highly qualified athletes and the denominator is that of lower qualified athletes.

Moving on to the correlational relationships in the men's 200m, indicators obtained over the course of recent years were higher than those recorded from the period of 1980 – 2000 (Table 1.2). Indeed, indicators of correlational relationships top out at 0.800 and this occurred 16 times in the recent years, compared to only 6 times in the earlier years. In addition, there were 26 occurrences of a 0.700 correlation in recent years and 20 in the previous years.

Table 1.2 – Indicators of correlational relationships for male 200m sprinters in several running exercises.

| Number | | 1 | 2 | 3 | 4 | 5 | 6 | 7 |
|---|---|---|---|---|---|---|---|---|
| | Exer. | 30m sprint stand. start | 60m sprint from blocks | 100m sprint from blocks | 150m sprint from blocks | 200m sprint from blocks | 300m sprint from blocks | 600m sprint from blocks |
| 1 | 30m sprint stand. start | – | 0.767 0.796 | 0.782 0.873 | 0.865 0.768 | 0.760 0.817 | 0.758 0.798 | 0.759 0.750 |
| 2 | 60m sprint from blocks | | – | 0.744 0.844 | 0.800 0.835 | 0.775 0.790 | 0.706 0.762 | 0.765 0.707 |
| 3 | 100m sprint from blocks | | | – | 0.824 0.789 | 0.776 0.800 | 0.783 0.756 | 0.757 0.707 |
| 4 | 150m sprint from blocks | | | | – | 0.886 0.853 | 0.805 0.806 | 0.814 0.787 |
| 5 | 200m sprint from blocks | | | | | – | 0.802 0.832 | 0.780 0.775 |
| 6 | 300m sprint from blocks | | | | | | – | 0.867 0.734 |
| 7 | 600m sprint from blocks | | | | | | | – |

Table 1.3 shows the results of correlational analysis in male 400m runners. These show a slight difference between runners in the two eras of sport that we are analyzing. First, a correlation of 0.800 was achieved 12 times in recent years and 15 in previous years. These are practically identical to the results in terms of the lowest correlation. Here are a few highlights:

| Correlation of various events to 400m male sprinters results, across decades | | |
|---|---|---|
| Event | 2000-2015 | 1980 - 2000 |
| 200 and 300m sprints | 0.878 | 0.872 |
| 400 and 600m sprints | 0.878 | 0.872 |
| 30m From blocks and 600m sprints | 0.576 | 0.550 |

Table 1.3 – Indicators of correlational relationships for male 400m sprinters in several running exercises.

| Number | | 1 | 2 | 3 | 4 | 5 | 6 | 7 |
|---|---|---|---|---|---|---|---|---|
| | Exer. | 30m sprint from blocks | 100m sprint from blocks | 150m sprint from blocks | 200m sprint from blocks | 300m sprint from blocks | 400m sprint from blocks | 600m sprint from blocks |
| 1 | 30m sprint from blocks | - | 0.862 0.810 | 0.802 0.777 | 0.755 0.768 | 0.702 0.783 | 0.665 0.607 | 0.624 0.550 |
| 2 | 100m sprint from blocks | | - | 0.864 0.804 | 0.821 0.787 | 0.768 0.740 | 0.707 0.725 | 0.660 0.602 |
| 3 | 150m sprint from blocks | | | - | 0.824 0.785 | 0.776 0.800 | 0.787 0.756 | 0.758 0.705 |
| 4 | 200m sprint from blocks | | | | - | 0.826 0.807 | 0.805 0.786 | 0.794 0.687 |
| 5 | 300m sprint from blocks | | | | | - | 0.832 0.832 | 0.785 0.676 |
| 6 | 400m sprint from blocks | | | | | | - | 0.872 0.839 |
| 7 | 600m sprint from blocks | | | | | | | - |

Table 1.4 shows the results of correlational analysis in the 110m hurdles. There is very little difference between these hurdle numbers and the data presented for the 400m. In 8 cases, the correlational analysis was 0.800 or higher (with 0.854 being the highest) in the earlier years and 6 cases (0.882) in recent years. The corresponding low numbers were 0.361 (30m sprint from blocks and 200m sprint), and 0.502 (for the same). In addition, the number of indicators that showed correlational relationships over 0.700 in the earlier years was 10 and in recent years, 17. There were several higher indicators of correlational association in athletes of the recent years and former years (Table 1.5), specializing in the 400m hurdles. In earlier years, higher correlations above 0.800 occurred 15 times (0.888 high) and in recent years, only 9 times (0.840 high). The corresponding low indicators were: 0.540 in the 60m hurdles with a 600m run and 0.350 in the 110m hurdles with 600m run.

Table 1.4 - Indicators of correlational relationships for male 110m hurdlers in various strength, jumping, and throwing exercises.

| Number | Exercise | Sports Results – Correlation Coefficient | | | | |
|--------|----------|--------------|--------------|--------------|--------------|--------------|
| | | 13.50 – 14.00 | 14.00 – 14.50 | 14.50 – 15.00 | 15.00 – 15.50 | 15.50 – 16.00 |
| 1 | Clean and Jerk | 0.490 | 0.443 | 0.400 | 0.381 | 0.356 |
| 2 | Half Squats (bar on back) | 0.400 | 0.393 | 0.345 | 0.360 | 0.356 |
| 3 | Broad jump w/med ball | 0.408 | 0.376 | 0.387 | 0.380 | 0.345 |
| 4 | Vertical Jump | 0.600 | 0.626 | 0.322 | 0.375 | 0.345 |
| 5 | Triple Jump w/med ball | 0.633 | 0.670 | 0.391 | 0.357 | 0.353 |
| 6 | 10-fold jumps w/med ball | 0.607 | 0.576 | 0.460 | 0.475 | 0.400 |
| 7 | 50m sprint | 0.645 | 0.652 | 0.564 | 0.457 | 0.400 |
| 8 | Shot throw forward | 0.276 | 0.245 | 0.266 | 0.309 | 0.208 |
| 9 | Shot throw backward | 0.311 | 0.289 | 0.320 | 0.260 | 0.275 |

Table 1.5 - Indicators of correlational relationships for male 400m hurdlers in various strength, jumping, and throwing exercises.

| Number | | 1 | 2 | 3 | 4 | 5 | 6 | 7 |
|--------|--------|---|---|---|---|---|---|---|
| | Exer. | 400m hurdle from blocks | 60m hurdle from blocks | 110m hurdle from blocks | 200m sprint from blocks | 400m sprint from blocks | 400m sprint stand. start | 600m sprint |
| 1 | 400m hurdles from blocks | - | 0.822 0.715 | 0.847 0.708 | 0.805 0.688 | 0.802 0.697 | 0.846 0.690 | 0.876 0.710 |
| 2 | 60m hurdles from blocks | | - | 0.834 0.774 | 0.821 0.696 | 0.770 0.683 | 0.629 0.624 | 0.540 0.565 |
| 3 | 110m hurdles from blocks | | | - | 0.794 0.697 | 0.803 0.707 | 0.700 0.656 | 0.659 0.632 |
| 4 | 200m sprint from blocks | | | | - | 0.817 0.716 | 0.784 0.737 | 0.615 0.688 |
| 5 | 400m sprint from blocks | | | | | - | 0.888 0.805 | 0.880 0.814 |
| 6 | 400m sprint stand. start | | | | | | - | 0.872 0.839 |
| 7 | 600m sprint stand. start | | | | | | | - |

Before we begin the work of analyzing the results of correlations between special developmental and competition exercises in groups of female sprinters, it is critical that we look at the data presented in Tables 1.6 – 1.10. These tables show correlational relationships obtained in experimental studies with athletes in the years from 2000 – 2010 in all sprinting disciplines and are compared to results of the same sport disciplines from the years between 1980 – 2000. This includes, not only correlation coefficients between 0.700 and higher, but also those in the range of 0.350 – 0.600. All of this speaks to the fact that, when compared to the data from the male groups, women's sprinting has undergone a positive shift in training methods. Making this assertion is important, but also quite complicated due to the fact that decades of athletes have gone through the track and field sprint system. In Table 1.6 you will find the results of correlational analysis for indicators of special-developmental and competition exercises in female 100m sprinters. These attest to the fact that there is a high level of correlation between most indicators examined. In 28 cases, the correlation coefficient was above 0.700 (up from only 16 occurrences from 1980 - 2000). In addition, the number of indicators that rose above 0.800 in the recent decade was 5 compared to 3 between 1980 and 2000. If most indicators of correlational relationship in athletes (female sprinters as shown in Table 1.6) of the earlier decades were shown for the 120 and 150m sprints, we would see a number of 0.882. This same level of correlational relationship in sprinters from 2000 – 2010 is seen in sprints of 150m and 600m. Indeed, many different indicators of correlational relationships were lower for athletes of the previous years. In comparing 30m sprints from blocks to 600m times, the previous decades scored 0.576 and the recent decade was 0.606.

Table 1.6 - Indicators of correlational relationships for female 100m sprinters in various running exercises.

| Number | | 1 | 2 | 3 | 4 | 5 | 6 | 7 |
|---|---|---|---|---|---|---|---|---|
| | Exer. | 30m sprint run. start | 30m sprint from blocks | 60m sprint from blocks | 100m sprint from blocks | 120m sprint from blocks | 150m sprint from blocks | 200m sprint from blocks |
| 1 | 30m sprint run. start | - | 0.723 0.756 | 0.742 0.815 | 0.715 0.801 | 0.666 0.724 | 0.709 0.697 | 0.720 0.680 |
| 2 | 30m sprint from blocks | | - | 0.746 0.798 | 0.730 0.673 | 0.747 0.766 | 0.606 0.677 | 0.687 0.702 |
| 3 | 60m sprint from blocks | | | - | 0.804 0.788 | 0.791 0.809 | 0.700 0.756 | 0.765 0.707 |
| 4 | 100m sprint from blocks | | | | - | 0.710 0.788 | 0.709 0.718 | 0.736 0.743 |
| 5 | 120m sprint from blocks | | | | | - | 0.775 0.798 | 0.789 0.762 |
| 6 | 150m sprint from blocks | | | | | | - | 0.882 0.753 |
| 7 | 200m sprint from blocks | | | | | | | - |

Table 1.7 shows the results of correlational analysis in 200m sprinters. In all cases, positive transfer between the exercises examined is observed. In athletes of the recent decade, 19 occurrences are observed where the correlation coefficient rises above 0.700 and 7 occurrences where it rises above 0.800. Data indicators for athletes from 1980-2000 show 12 occurrences over 0.700 and 1 case over 0.800. This shift is also observed in other indicators as well. For example, in most indicators of correlational relationship in athletes from the previous years, we see a 0.803 relationship between 300m and 600m sprints and a 0.880 correlation between 150m and 200m sprints. Some of the lowest indicators for this group are a 0.468 between 150m and 600m sprints and have the same correlation between a 60m from the blocks and a 600m sprint.

Table 1.7 - Indicators of correlational relationships for female 200m sprinters in various running exercises.

| Number | | 1 | 2 | 3 | 4 | 5 | 6 | 7 |
|---|---|---|---|---|---|---|---|---|
| | Exer. | 30m sprint run. start | 60m sprint from blocks | 100m sprint from blocks | 150m sprint from blocks | 200m sprint from blocks | 300m sprint from blocks | 400m sprint from blocks |
| 1 | 30m sprint run. start | - | 0.702 0.696 | 0.682 0.775 | 0.665 0.718 | 0.760 0.711 | 0.658 0.598 | 0.555 0.550 |
| 2 | 60m sprint from blocks | | - | 0.740 0.743 | 0.707 0.736 | 0.718 0.700 | 0.606 0.561 | 0.563 0.402 |
| 3 | 100m sprint from blocks | | | - | 0.804 0.748 | 0.785 0.720 | 0.689 0.656 | 0.558 0.400 |
| 4 | 150m sprint from blocks | | | | - | 0.885 0.824 | 0.866 0.765 | 0.714 0.708 |
| 5 | 200m sprint from blocks | | | | | - | 0.812 0.800 | 0.783 0.876 |
| 6 | 300m sprint from blocks | | | | | | - | 0.852 0.787 |
| 7 | 400m sprint from blocks | | | | | | | - |

Particular interest is sparked by the results of correlational analysis in 200m sprints (Table 1.8). Here the number of cases rising above 0.700 and 0.800 was higher in athletes of the recent decade, 31, compared to 27 in the previous years. In athletes from the 1980-2000 time period, correlational analysis was done between sprints of 150m and 200m but in current athletes this was done between sprints of 400m and 600m.

Table 1.8 - Indicators of correlational relationships for female 400m sprinters in various running exercises.

| Number | | 1 | 2 | 3 | 4 | 5 | 6 | 7 |
|---|---|---|---|---|---|---|---|---|
| | Exer. | 60m sprint from blocks | 100m sprint from blocks | 150m sprint from blocks | 200m sprint from blocks | 300m sprint run. start | 400m sprint from blocks | 600m sprint from blocks |
| 1 | 60m sprint from blocks | - | 0.765 0.800 | 0.702 0.798 | 0.656 0.774 | 0.642 0.700 | 0.655 0.626 | 0.604 0.590 |
| 2 | 100m sprint from blocks | | - | 0.804 0.816 | 0.823 0.793 | 0.774 0.734 | 0.677 0.729 | 0.630 0.622 |
| 3 | 150m sprint from blocks | | | - | 0.814 0.876 | 0.795 0.831 | 0.767 0.746 | 0.708 0.697 |
| 4 | 200m sprint from blocks | | | | - | 0.808 0.796 | 0.793 0.809 | 0.774 0.708 |
| 5 | 300m sprint running start | | | | | - | 0.845 0.812 | 0.880 0.777 |
| 6 | 400m sprint from blocks | | | | | | - | 0.892 0.805 |
| 7 | 600m sprint from blocks | | | | | | | - |

In Table 1.9, we see the results of correlational analysis for preparation between special-developmental and competition exercises in the 110m hurdles; These show a high level of correlation between one another. In athletes from the earlier decades, 21 cases rose above a 0.700 correlation and 8 were over 0.800 compared to the athletes from recent years who had 17 over 0.700 and 14 over 0.800. The highest correlated exercises for athletes of previous years was between a 60m sprint from the blocks and the 100m dash at 0.865. For athletes of the more recent decade, the highest correlation was observed between 100m sprints and 150m sprints at 0.888. On the other hand, the lowest indicators for the analysis of these four exercises was 0.365 and 0.566, respectively.

Table 1.9 - Indicators of correlational relationships for female 100m hurdlers in various running exercises.

| Number | | 1 | 2 | 3 | 4 | 5 | 6 | 7 |
|---|---|---|---|---|---|---|---|---|
| | Exer. | 100m hurdles from blocks | 60m hurdles from blocks | 30m sprint from blocks | 60m sprint from blocks | 100m sprint from blocks | 150m sprint run. start | 200m sprint from blocks |
| 1 | 100m hurdles from blocks | - | 0.860 0.804 | 0.723 0.769 | 0.736 0.768 | 0.707 0.800 | 0.728 0.713 | 0.564 0.585 |
| 2 | 60m hurdles from blocks | | - | 0.800 0.790 | 0.794 0.783 | 0.785 0.710 | 0.692 0.645 | 0.633 0.602 |
| 3 | 30m sprint from blocks | | | - | 0.862 0.806 | 0.767 0.750 | 0.712 0.698 | 0.565 0.600 |
| 4 | 60m sprint from blocks | | | | - | 0.846 0.876 | 0.791 0.718 | 0.714 0.603 |
| 5 | 100m sprint from blocks | | | | | - | 0.888 0.861 | 0.756 0.646 |
| 6 | 150m sprint run. start | | | | | | - | 0.762 0.757 |
| 7 | 200m sprint from blocks | | | | | | | - |

In Table 1.10, we see the results of correlational analysis in the 400m hurdles. In athletes of the previous decade, indicators over 0.700 occurred 12 times, in addition to 6 times over 0.800. For athletes of the more recent decade, 16 occurrences rose over 0.700 and 12 over 0.800. The best results for the previous group were between the 60m sprint from blocks and the 100m dash. In the more recent group, the highest indicators were between the 400m hurdles and the 600m sprint.

Table 1.10 - Indicators of correlational relationships for female 400m hurdlers in various running exercises.

| Number | | 1 | 2 | 3 | 4 | 5 | 6 | 7 |
|---|---|---|---|---|---|---|---|---|
| | Exer. | 400m hurdles from blocks | 60m hurdles from blocks | 100m hurdles from blocks | 200m sprint from blocks | 300m sprint from blocks | 400m sprint run. start | 600m sprint run. start |
| 1 | 400m hurdles from blocks | - | 0.723 0.790 | 0.782 0.763 | 0.814 0.761 | 0.800 0.720 | 0.867 0.692 | 0.880 0.770 |
| 2 | 60m hurdles from blocks | | - | 0.884 0.805 | 0.809 0.764 | 0.782 0.789 | 0.705 0.603 | 0.676 0.502 |
| 3 | 100m hurdles from blocks | | | - | 0.763 0.678 | 0.600 0.715 | 0.570 0.554 | 0.613 0.455 |
| 4 | 200m sprint from blocks | | | | - | 0.768 0.726 | 0.727 0.706 | 0.665 0.588 |
| 5 | 300m sprint from blocks | | | | | - | 0.814 0.792 | 0.855 0.804 |
| 6 | 400m sprint run. start | | | | | | - | 0.851 0.838 |
| 7 | 600m sprint run. start | | | | | | | - |

Tables 1.11 – 1.13 show the results of correlational analysis in sprinters from the 100, 200, and 400m events. Positive training transfer was observed on all levels of sports mastery in each jumping exercise. In addition, the highest correlation coefficient was observed in the tenfold jumps with a standing start and single leg jumps in series. There is also positive transfer observed in two throwing exercises: shot throws forward and shot throws backward. If, in a 100m sprinter, there was positive correlation observed for the snatch on two levels of sports results (11.10 – 11.40 and 11.40 – 11.70) then you might see transfer for 400m sprinters in the second and third levels of sports mastery and there might be transfer for the 400m athletes running the slowest times (22.50 – 23.00).  On all levels of sports mastery there is a place for positive transfer in 100m sprinters with a half squat, but for 200m sprinters it only transfers for the slowest athletes, and for 400m sprinters, for the two slowest categories. In 110m and 400m hurdlers (Table 1.15), positive transfer is observed on all levels of sports mastery in tenfold jumps with a standing start and single leg continuous bounding for 50m. In all the other strength and running exercises, in 400m sprinters, we see positive transfer on all levels of sports mastery. Positive transfer is observed for 110m hurdlers in the clean for the three first groups, the half squat for the first two groups, in long jump for the first group, in vertical jumps for the first two groups, and in triple jumps for the first three groups.

When we compare the given results of correlational analysis in Tables 1.11 – 1.15 from research over the course of the most recent decade (2000-2010) to data from the previous two decades, we see that they differ significantly. There is only one area of sports training where there is no difference between the two time periods – throwing exercises. In all other exercises there is a large difference on all levels of sports mastery. For example, we will take a look at positive training transfer in 200m sprinters. In the clean and the vertical jump, there is not one level of sports mastery where we observe positive training transfer. In the other exercises, transfer is greatest for those athletes who are already running in the fastest category.

Table 1.11 – Indicators of correlational relationships for preparatory exercises in male 100m sprinters in several strength, jumping, and throwing exercises.

| Number | Exercise | Sports Results – Correlation Coefficient | | | | |
|---|---|---|---|---|---|---|
| | | 10.20-10.50 sec | 10.50-10.80 sec | 10.80-11.10 sec | 11.10-11.40 sec | 11.40-11.70 sec |
| 1 | Clean and Jerk | 0.235 | 0.298 | 0.350 | 0.457 | 0.400 |
| 2 | Half Squats (bar on back) | 0.400 | 0.435 | 0.456 | 0.427 | 0.586 |
| 3 | Broad jump w/med ball | 0.466 | 0.446 | 0.561 | 0.568 | 0.497 |
| 4 | Vertical Jump | 0.650 | 0.635 | 0.564 | 0.524 | 0.560 |
| 5 | Triple Jump w/ball | 0.634 | 0.677 | 0.543 | 0.490 | 0.400 |
| 6 | 10-fold jumps w/ ball | 0.764 | 0 725 | 0.600 | 0.543 | 0.500 |
| 7 | 50m sprint | 0.734 | 0.741 | 0.655 | 0.600 | 0.483 |
| 8 | Forward shot throw | 0.367 | 0.360 | 0.360 | 0.321 | 0.306 |
| 9 | Backward shot throw | 0.356 | 0.377 | 0.342 | 0.324 | 0. 361 |

Table 1.12 – Indicators of correlational relationships for preparatory exercises in male 200m sprinters in several strength, jumping, and throwing exercises.

| Number | Exercise | Sports Results – Correlation Coefficient | | | | |
|---|---|---|---|---|---|---|
| | | 20.50-21.00 sec | 21.00-21.50 sec | 21.50 – 22.00 sec | 22.00 – 22.50 sec | 22.50 – 23.00 sec |
| 1 | Clean and Jerk | 0.370 | 0.365 | 0.300 | 0.353 | 0.410 |
| 2 | Half Squats (bar on back) | 0.671 | 0.634 | 0.600 | 0.415 | 0.388 |
| 3 | Broad jump w/med ball | 0.566 | 0.533 | 0.500 | 0.562 | 0.403 |
| 4 | Vertical Jump | 0.630 | 0.665 | 0.604 | 0.563 | 0.460 |
| 5 | Triple Jump w/ball | 0.734 | 0.787 | 0.625 | 0.570 | 0.410 |
| 6 | 10-fold jumps w/ ball | 0.784 | 0.783 | 0.710 | 0.641 | 0.577 |
| 7 | 50m sprint | 0.804 | 0.781 | 0.750 | 0.549 | 0.415 |
| 8 | Forward shot throw | 0.312 | 0.333 | 0.350 | 0.338 | 0.375 |
| 9 | Backward shot throw | 0.372 | 0.365 | 0.340 | 0.317 | 0. 346 |

Table 1.13 – Indicators of correlational relationships for preparatory exercises in male 400m sprinters in several strength, jumping, and throwing exercises.

| Number | Exercise | Sports Results – Correlation Coefficient | | | | |
|--------|----------|------------------|------------------|------------------|------------------|------------------|
| | | 46.00 – 47.00 sec | 47.00 – 48.00 sec | 48.00 – 49.00 sec | 49.00 – 50.00 sec | 50.00-51.00 sec |
| 1 | Clean and Jerk | 0.391 | 0.400 | 0.365 | 0.384 | 0.376 |
| 2 | Half Squats (bar on back) | 0.573 | 0.612 | 0.508 | 0.407 | 0.378 |
| 3 | Broad jump w/med ball | 0.466 | 0.511 | 0.430 | 0.485 | 0.423 |
| 4 | Vertical Jump | 0.690 | 0.657 | 0.623 | 0.662 | 0.424 |
| 5 | Triple Jump w/ball | 0.834 | 0.753 | 0.672 | 0.597 | 0.412 |
| 6 | 10-fold jumps w/ ball | 0.808 | 0 785 | 0.760 | 0.633 | 0.432 |
| 7 | 50m sprint | 0.832 | 0.802 | 0.761 | 0.657 | 0.432 |
| 8 | Forward shot throw | 0.305 | 0.360 | 0.287 | 0.353 | 0.302 |
| 9 | Backward shot throw | 0.364 | 0.309 | 0.322 | 0.273 | 0.286 |

Table 1.14 – Indicators of correlational relationships for preparatory exercises in male 110m hurdlers in several strength, jumping, and throwing exercises.

| Number | Exercise | Sports Results – Correlation Coefficient | | | | |
|--------|----------|-----------|-----------|-----------|-----------|-----------|
| | | 13.50 – 14.00 sec | 14.00 – 14.50 sec | 14.50 – 15.00 sec | 15.00 – 15.50 sec | 15.00 – 15.50 sec |
| 1 | Clean and Jerk | 0.490 | 0.443 | 0.400 | 0.381 | 0.356 |
| 2 | Half Squats (bar on back) | 0.400 | 0.393 | 0.345 | 0.360 | 0.356 |
| 3 | Broad jump w/med ball | 0.408 | 0.376 | 0.387 | 0.380 | 0.345 |
| 4 | Vertical Jump | 0.600 | 0.626 | 0.322 | 0.375 | 0.345 |
| 5 | Triple Jump w/ball | 0.633 | 0.670 | 0.391 | 0.357 | 0.353 |
| 6 | 10-fold jumps w/ ball | 0.607 | 0 576 | 0.460 | 0.475 | 0. 400 |
| 7 | 50m sprint | 0.645 | 0.652 | 0.564 | 0.457 | 0.400 |
| 8 | Forward shot throw | 0.276 | 0.245 | 0.266 | 0.309 | 0.208 |
| 9 | Backward shot throw | 0.311 | 0.289 | 0.320 | 0.260 | 0.265 |

Table 1.15 – Indicators of correlational relationships for preparatory exercises in male 400m hurdlers in several strength, jumping, and throwing exercises.

| Number | Exercise | Sports Results – Correlation Coefficient | | | | |
|---|---|---|---|---|---|---|
| | | 49.50 – 50.50 sec | 50.50 – 51.50 sec | 51.50 – 52.50 sec | 52.50 – 53.50 sec | 53.50 – 54.50 sec |
| 1 | Clean and Jerk | 0.388 | 0.377 | 0.341 | 0.307 | 0.312 |
| 2 | Half Squats (bar on back) | 0.370 | 0.324 | 0.313 | 0.307 | 0.355 |
| 3 | Broad jump w/med ball | 0.378 | 0.371 | 0.360 | 0.325 | 0.309 |
| 4 | Vertical Jump | 0.300 | 0.375 | 0.346 | 0.347 | 0.303 |
| 5 | Triple Jump w/ball | 0.376 | 0.380 | 0.334 | 0.351 | 0.333 |
| 6 | 10-fold jumps w/ ball | 0.532 | 0 588 | 0.452 | 0.409 | 0. 437 |
| 7 | 50m sprint | 0.606 | 0.587 | 0.555 | 0.487 | 0.430 |
| 8 | Forward shot throw | 0.256 | 0.205 | 0.243 | 0.208 | 0.200 |
| 9 | Backward shot throw | 0.289 | 0.315 | 0.306 | 0.275 | 0.203 |

Tables 1.16 – 1.20 show the results of correlational data that analyze female sprinters. Aside from a few details (which we will talk about later) two facts are apparent: First, on all levels of sports mastery in each type of female sprints, there is a positive transfer between indicators of throwing the shot forward and back. There is also a positive transfer for tenfold jumps from a standing start and alternate leg bounding for 50m. In the 100m hurdles there is a positive correlational relationship in the triple jump for athletes in the 12.80-13.30 second class. In this exercise, on all levels of sports mastery, there is a positive correlational relationship for the 100m sprinters, but for 200m sprints it is only observed in athletes who run between 23.50-25.50sec. In one of the strength exercises (squats) we observe positive correlational relationships in only 100m sprinters who can run between 11.20-11.80. In the other jumping exercises, 200m sprinters who run between 23.50-25.50sec saw a positive transfer for the vertical jump along with 100m sprinters in the 12.20-12.70sec range. In the other two levels of sports mastery (12.10-12.40, 12.40-12.70) we observed a positive transfer for the broad jump from a standing start.

Table 1.16 – Indicators of correlational relationships for preparatory exercises in female 100m sprinters in several strength, jumping, and throwing exercises.

| Number | Exercise | Sports Results – Correlation Coefficient | | | | |
|---|---|---|---|---|---|---|
| | | 11.20 – 11.50 sec | 11.50- 11.80 sec | 11.80 -12.10 sec | 12.10 – 12.40 sec | 12.40 – 12.70 sec |
| 1 | Clean and Jerk | 0.342 | 0.299 | 0.330 | 0.344 | 0.383 |
| 2 | Half Squats (bar on back) | 0.420 | 0.396 | 0.345 | 0.324 | 0.311 |
| 3 | Broad jump w/med ball | 0.345 | 0.376 | 0.324 | 0.403 | 0.390 |
| 4 | Vertical Jump | 0.388 | 0.345 | 0.375 | 0.444 | 0.405 |
| 5 | Triple Jump w/ball | 0.396 | 0.423 | 0.452 | 0.431 | 0.409 |
| 6 | 10-fold jumps w/ ball | 0.568 | 0.487 | 0.407 | 0.465 | 0.428 |
| 7 | 50m sprint | 0.568 | 0.580 | 0.508 | 0.457 | 0.465 |
| 8 | Forward shot throw | 0.243 | 0.287 | 0.290 | 0.243 | 0.314 |
| 9 | Backward shot throw | 0.332 | 0.305 | 0.324 | 0.298 | 0. 324 |

Table 1.17 – Indicators of correlational relationships for preparatory exercises in female 200m sprinters in several strength, jumping, and throwing exercises.

| Number | Exercise | Sports Results – Correlation Coefficient | | | | |
|---|---|---|---|---|---|---|
| | | 22.70 – 23.00 sec | 23.00 – 23.50 sec | 23.50 – 24.00 sec | 24.00 – 24.50 sec | 25.00 – 25.50 sec |
| 1 | Clean and Jerk | 0.305 | 0.288 | 0.313 | 0.346 | 0.342 |
| 2 | Half Squats (bar on back) | 0.277 | 0.342 | 0.323 | 0.309 | 0.306 |
| 3 | Broad jump standing start | 0.366 | 0.325 | 0.312 | 0.315 | 0.346 |
| 4 | Vertical Jump | 0.375 | 0.370 | 0.407 | 0.394 | 0.413 |
| 5 | Triple Jump standing start | 0.365 | 0.357 | 0.398 | 0.407 | 0.405 |
| 6 | 10-fold jumps standing start | 0.486 | 0.507 | 0.465 | 0.490 | 0.456 |
| 7 | 50m sprint | 0.506 | 0.506 | 0.468 | 0.500 | 0.476 |
| 8 | Forward shot throw | 0.276 | 0.311 | 0.287 | 0.343 | 0.304 |
| 9 | Backward shot throw | 0.308 | 0.375 | 0.343 | 0.300 | 0. 342 |

Table 1.18 – Indicators of correlational relationships for preparatory exercises in female 400m sprinters in several strength, jumping, and throwing exercises.

| Number | Exercise | Sports Results – Correlation Coefficient | | | | |
|---|---|---|---|---|---|---|
| | | 50.00 – 51.00 sec | 51.00– 52.00 sec | 52.00– 53.00 sec | 53.00 – 54.00 sec | 55.00 – 55.00 sec |
| 1 | Clean and Jerk | 0.340 | 0.313 | 0.356 | 0.312 | 0.298 |
| 2 | Half Squats (bar on back) | 0.197 | 0.278 | 0.317 | 0.365 | 0.321 |
| 3 | Broad jump standing start | 0.278 | 0.345 | 0.380 | 0.354 | 0.376 |
| 4 | Vertical Jump | 0.309 | 0.298 | 0.376 | 0.306 | 0.357 |
| 5 | Triple Jump standing start | 0.365 | 0.321 | 0.376 | 0.306 | 0.357 |
| 6 | 10-fold jumps standing start | 0.566 | 0.587 | 0.506 | 0.487 | 0.438 |
| 7 | 50m sprint | 0.577 | 0.532 | 0.500 | 0.467 | 0.417 |
| 8 | Forward shot throw | 0.204 | 0.265 | 0.232 | 0.309 | 0.344 |
| 9 | Backward shot throw | 0.300 | 0.276 | 0.311 | 0.290 | 0.253 |

Table 1.19 – Indicators of correlational relationships for preparatory exercises in female 100m hurdlers in several strength, jumping, and throwing exercises.

| Number | Exercise | Sports Results – Coefficient Correlation | | | | |
|---|---|---|---|---|---|---|
| | | 12.80 – 13.30 sec | 13.30– 13.80 sec | 13.80– 14.30 0 sec | 14.30 – 14.80 sec | 14.80 – 15.30 sec |
| 1 | Clean and Jerk | 0.345 | 0.312 | 0.300 | 0.319 | 0.343 |
| 2 | Half Squats (bar on back) | 0.300 | 0.293 | 0.321 | 0.339 | 0.288 |
| 3 | Broad jump standing start | 0.344 | 0.321 | 0.278 | 0.300 | 0.346 |
| 4 | Vertical Jump | 0.289 | 0.325 | 0.287 | 0.300 | 0.343 |
| 5 | Triple Jump standing start | 0.414 | 0.385 | 0.357 | 0.356 | 0.324 |
| 6 | 10-fold jumps standing start | 0.486 | 0.409 | 0.400 | 0.432 | 0.397 |
| 7 | 50m sprint | 0.456 | 0.502 | 0.409 | 0.434 | 0.425 |
| 8 | Forward shot throw | 0.200 | 0.223 | 0.198 | 0.210 | 0.213 |
| 9 | Backward shot throw | 0.278 | 0.267 | 0.300 | 0.232 | 0.198 |

Table 1.20 – Indicators of correlational relationships for preparatory exercises in female 400m hurdlers in several strength, jumping, and throwing exercises.

| Number | Exercise | Sports Results – Coefficient Correlation | | | | |
|---|---|---|---|---|---|---|
| | | 54.00 – 55.00 sec | 55.00– 56.00 sec | 56.00– 57.00 sec | 57.00 – 58.00 sec | 58.00 – 59.00 sec |
| 1 | Clean and Jerk | 0.268 | 0.302 | 0.277 | 0.314 | 0.287 |
| 2 | Half Squats (bar on back) | 0.288 | 0.307 | 0.245 | 0.334 | 0.290 |
| 3 | Broad jump standing start | 0.290 | 0.267 | 0.310 | 0.317 | 0.276 |
| 4 | Vertical Jump | 0.286 | 0.305 | 0.267 | 0.332 | 0.265 |
| 5 | Triple Jump standing start | 0.308 | 0.344 | 0.303 | 0.304 | 0.317 |
| 6 | 10-fold jumps standing start | 0.408 | 0.387 | 0.412 | 0.414 | 0.390 |
| 7 | 50m sprint | 0.561 | 0.509 | 0.502 | 0.446 | 0.401 |
| 8 | Forward shot throw | 0.200 | 0.187 | 0.256 | 0.233 | 0.244 |
| 9 | Backward shot throw | 0.224 | 0.206 | 0.298 | 0.206 | 0.198 |

Table 1.21 shows the best (1) and worst (2) results of male 100m sprinters of varying sport qualification for two strength, three jumping, and one throwing exercise. These demonstrate the fact that, in all cases, the greatest sports results are shown by athletes in the first level of sports mastery (10.20 – 10.50 seconds) and the worst are shown in the last level (11.40 – 11.80 seconds). A similar relationship is not observed when comparing between the best and worst results across all levels of sports mastery. For example, in the snatch, on the first level of sports mastery, the difference is 22.5kg and in the last, 15kg.  In addition, a large difference is observed in the jumping exercises. For example, on the first level of sports mastery in the long jump, the best result is 30cm further than the worst and in the lowest level of sports mastery, the difference between best and worst performances is 17cm.

Table 1.21 – Comparison of characteristics for the best (1) and worst (2) results for male 100m sprinters in several strength, jumping, and throwing exercises.

| Exercise | | Sports Results | | | | |
|---|---|---|---|---|---|---|
| | | 10.20 – 10.50 sec | 10.50 – 10.80 sec | 10.80– 11.10 sec | 11.10 – 11.40 sec | 11.40 – 11.70 sec |
| Snatch (kg) | 1 | 90 | 85 | 82.5 | 82.5 | 80 |
| | 2 | 67.5 | 67.5 | 60 | 67.5 | 65 |
| Half Squats (bar on back) (kg) | 1 | 200 | 185 | 180 | 180 | 170 |
| | 2 | 155 | 155 | 145 | 140 | 130 |
| Broad jump standing start (cm) | 1 | 325 | 321 | 316 | 312 | 305 |
| | 2 | 295 | 287 | 291 | 285 | 287 |
| Vertical Jump (cm) | 1 | 87 | 87 | 84 | 86 | 80 |
| | 2 | 66 | 63 | 62 | 61 | 59 |
| Triple Jump standing start (cm) | 1 | 967 | 941 | 913 | 920 | 902 |
| | 2 | | | | | |
| Forward shot Throw (m) | 1 | 16.95 | 16.50 | 16.79 | 16.23 | 16.25 |
| | 2 | 15.66 | 15.73 | 15.88 | 15.54 | 15.23 |

In Table 1.22, the best and worst results for male 200m sprinters are shown. Here we again observe a tendency towards better results for those participants of higher sport qualification. In at least two cases, each of the following levels of sports mastery's results are slightly lower than the previous level. The most impressive results were observed in the difference between the best and worst results. Among these strength exercises, the difference varies between 15-30kg. In the standing broad jump, the difference is between 20-29cm, for the vertical jump, 22-25cm, for the triple jump, 18-37cm, and in forward shot throws, 67-102cm.

In general, the level of the best and worst strength, jumping, and speed indicators for athletes in the 400m were lower than the athletes who competed in shorter distance events (Table 1.23). There is also a smaller difference between the best and worst indicators for these groups. For example, in the snatch, the difference is from 15-27.5kg and in the forward shot throw it is from 69-102cm. In most cases a tendency is observed that indicator exercises will be worse as sports mastery decreases.

Table 1.22 – Comparison of characteristics for the best (1) and worst (2) results in male 200m sprinters in several strength, jumping, and throwing exercises.

| Exercise | | Sports Results | | | | |
|---|---|---|---|---|---|---|
| | | 20.50 – 21.00 sec | 21.00 – 21.50 sec | 21.50– 22.00 sec | 22.00 – 22.50 sec | 22.50 – 23.00 sec |
| Clean and Jerk (kg) | 1 2 | 80 65 | 82.5 60 | 77.5 60 | 80 57.5 | 75 55 |
| Half Squats (bar on back) (kg) | 1 2 | 180 155 | 180 165 | 170 140 | 165 135 | 155 130 |
| Broad jump standing start (cm) | 1 2 | 315 290 | 316 285 | 310 290 | 309 281 | 300 280 |
| Vertical Jump (cm) | 1 2 | 88 67 | 84 63 | 82 60 | 80 62 | 71 53 |
| Triple Jump standing start (cm) | 1 2 | 943 905 | 925 907 | 906 885 | 900 864 | 893 873 |
| Forward shot Throw (m) | 1 2 | 16.77 15.88 | 16.70 15.97 | 16.66 15.64 | 16.76 15.83 | 16.43 15.76 |

Table 1.23 – Comparison of characteristics for the best (1) and worst (2) results in male 400m sprinters in several strength, jumping, and throwing exercises.

| Exercise | | Sports Results | | | | |
|---|---|---|---|---|---|---|
| | | 46.00 – 47.00 sec | 47.00 – 48.00 sec | 48.00– 49.00 sec | 49.00 – 50.00 sec | 50.00 – 51.00 sec |
| Clean and Jerk (kg) | 1 | 75 | 75 | 70 | 65 | 67.5 |
| | 2 | 60 | 57.5 | 55 | 52.5 | 50 |
| Half Squats (bar on back) (kg) | 1 | 165 | 170 | 165 | 165 | 150 |
| | 2 | 135 | 135 | 130 | 135 | 130 |
| Broad jump standing start (cm) | 1 | 310 | 306 | 300 | 296 | 290 |
| | 2 | 287 | 280 | 280 | 282 | 275 |
| Vertical Jump (cm) | 1 | 80 | 79 | 75 | 80 | 69 |
| | 2 | 65 | 64 | 61 | 63 | 56 |
| Triple Jump standing start (cm) | 1 | 923 | 909 | 900 | 880 | 875 |
| | 2 | 890 | 876 | 870 | 856 | 855 |
| Forward shot Throw (m) | 1 | 16.80 | 16.66 | 16.50 | 16.36 | 16.40 |
| | 2 | 16.00 | 15.85 | 15.87 | 15.45 | 15.76 |

Table 1.24 – Comparison of characteristics for the best (1) and worst (2) results in male 110m hurdlers in several strength, jumping, and throwing exercises.

| Exercise | | Sports Results | | | | |
|---|---|---|---|---|---|---|
| | | 13.50 – 14.00 sec | 14.00 – 14.50 sec | 14.50– 15.00 sec | 15.00 – 15.50 sec | 15.50 – 16.00 sec |
| Clean and Jerk (kg) | 1 2 | 77.5 60 | 75 60 | 72.5 57.5 | 72.50 55 | 67.5 52.5 |
| Half Squats (bar on back) (kg) | 1 2 | 170 145 | 170 140 | 165 130 | 160 135 | 152.5 130 |
| Broad jump standing start (cm) | 1 2 | 317 289 | 320 294 | 315 280 | 305 276 | 295 273 |
| Vertical Jump (cm) | 1 2 | 85 67 | 80 63 | 75 61 | 70 57 | 65 52 |
| Triple Jump standing start (cm) | 1 2 | 934 880 | 916 870 | 921 886 | 900 975 | 889 866 |
| Forward shot Throw (m) | 1 2 | 16.70 16.21 | 16.79 15.99 | 16.44 15.83 | 16.50 15.66 | 16.46 15.78 |

Table 1.25 – Comparison of characteristics for the best (1) and worst (2) results in male 400m hurdlers in several strength, jumping, and throwing exercises.

| Exercise | | Sports Results | | | | |
|---|---|---|---|---|---|---|
| | | 49.50 – 50.50 sec | 50.50 – 51.50 sec | 51.50– 52.50 sec | 52.50 – 53.50 sec | 53.50 – 54.50 sec |
| Clean and Jerk (kg) | 1 | 72.5 | 72.5 | 72.5 | 70 | 67.5 |
| | 2 | 60 | 62.5 | 57.5 | 55 | 50 |
| Half Squats (bar on back) (kg) | 1 | 160 | 165 | 160 | 150 | 140 |
| | 2 | 145 | 140 | 135 | 130 | 125 |
| Broad jump standing start (cm) | 1 | 307 | 300 | 305 | 300 | 297 |
| | 2 | 280 | 284 | 280 | 270 | 267 |
| Vertical Jump (cm) | 1 | 80 | 72 | 70 | 68 | 64 |
| | 2 | 59 | 55 | 54 | 50 | 47 |
| Triple Jump standing start (cm) | 1 | 920 | 911 | 900 | 890 | 878 |
| | 2 | 890 | 880 | 875 | 866 | 848 |
| Forward shot Throw (m) | 1 | 16.60 | 16.48 | 16.12 | 16.51 | 1632 |
| | 2 | 16.27 | 15.65 | 15.54 | 15.35 | 15.46 |

Tables 1.26-1.30 show the best and worst results for five levels of sports mastery that represent female athletes who specialize in hurdle events. These charts examine several strength, jumping, and running exercises. We will begin with strength indicators. In the snatch, on 3 occasions (200m, 110m hurdles, and 400m hurdles) the difference

between the best and worst results for the aforementioned levels of sports mastery did not rise above 10kg. Only in one case (100m sprinters) is the difference slightly lower: 15kg to 25kg. Concerning the worst results, we will look at the following indicators: 100m sprints – 5kg, 200m – 2.5kg, 400m – 7.5kg, 100m hurdles – 10kg, 400m hurdles - 12.5kg. The largest difference was observed in the squat with athletes who competed in the 100m hurdles - 20kg (best result). In this group the difference from here to the worst result was 15kg less weight. In three cases (100m sprint, 200m and 400m hurdles) the difference between the best and worst result was 10kg. In the 400m, the best and worst results were identical. The difference between indicators for the worst results in the 100, 200, and 400m hurdles are respectively: 20kg, 2.5kg, and 12.5kg.

Now we will look at what type of differences were observed for the best and worst results for the standing long jump. In athletes who compete in the 200m, the difference between the best and worst jumps was 28cm. In the 400m hurdles – 19cm, in the 100m – 18cm, in the 400m – 17cm. The difference between the worst results: 100m hurdles – 26cm, 200m and 400 hurdles – 22 cm, 100m – 21cm, and 400m – 15cm.

Completely different numbers were shown between the best and worst results in the vertical jump. Here the difference between them reached 4cm in only one case – the 200m sprinters. In the rest of the cases, the difference fluctuated between 1cm and 2cm. The greatest difference between the best and worst results were observed in the triple jump. This, given the specific nature of this exercise, makes it much different than any of the other jumping exercise (broad jump and vertical jump). The difference between the best indicators in the 100, 200, 400, and 100 and 400 hurdles was (respectively): 27, 22, 31, 35 and 36cm, and the difference between the worst: 22, 57, 36, 59, and 44 cm. It becomes clear, based on correlational analysis, that on all levels of sports mastery, there was not one case where the forward shot throw produced a positive training transfer. This could be explained by the differences in the best and worst results. These were all significantly overwhelming in most cases. Beginning with the difference between the best results: 100m – 27cm, 200m – 104cm, 400m – 31cm, 100m hurdles – 35cm, and 400 hurdles – 36cm. For the worst results: 100m – 22cm, 200m -26cm, 400m – 36cm, 100m hurdles – 59cm, 400m hurdles – 44cm.

Aside from a few outlier data points (from Tables 1.26 and 1.30), we can reasonably assume that there is a significant relationship between indicator exercise performance and the level of sports mastery achieved by the athlete and thus a significant difference between indicator performances by athletes of different qualification.

Table 1.26 – Comparison of characteristics for the best (1) and worst (2) results in female 100m sprinters in several strength, jumping, and throwing exercises.

| Exercise | | Sports Results | | | | |
|---|---|---|---|---|---|---|
| | | 11.20 – 11.50 sec | 11.50 – 11.80 sec | 11.80– 12.10 sec | 12.10 – 12.40 sec | 12.40 – 12.70 sec |
| Clean and Jerk (kg) | 1 2 | 65 45 | 60 45 | 60 40 | 55 40 | 55 40 |
| Half Squats (bar on back) (kg) | 1 2 | 140 115 | 130 110 | 130 105 | 125 100 | 120 95 |
| Broad jump standing start (cm) | 1 2 | 278 251 | 267 244 | 266 230 | 267 245 | 260 241 |
| Vertical Jump (cm) | 1 2 | 62 47 | 63 45 | 60 40 | 58 40 | 54 41 |
| Triple Jump standing start (cm) | 1 2 | 843 812 | 834 807 | 820 789 | 826 780 | 816 785 |
| Forward shot Throw (m) | 1 2 | 14.76 14.12 | 14.23 13.87 | 14.56 13.90 | 14.07 13.90 | 14.15 13.69 |

Table 1.27 – Comparison of characteristics for the best (1) and worst (2) results in female 200m sprinters in several strength, jumping, and throwing exercises.

| Exercise | | Sports Results | | | | |
|---|---|---|---|---|---|---|
| | | 22.70 – 23.00 sec | 23.00 – 23.50 sec | 23.50– 24.00 sec | 24.00 – 24.50 sec | 24.50 – 25.00 sec |
| Clean and Jerk (kg) | 1<br>2 | 60<br>40 | 57.5<br>40 | 57.5<br>40 | 50<br>37.5 | 50<br>40 |
| Half Squats (bar on back) (kg) | 1<br>2 | 135<br>100 | 140<br>110 | 130<br>100 | 115<br>90 | 110<br>90 |
| Broad jump standing start (cm) | 1<br>2 | 263<br>224 | 260<br>232 | 255<br>241 | 241<br>228 | 235<br>219 |
| Vertical Jump (cm) | 1<br>2 | 65<br>47 | 61<br>45 | 60<br>48 | 57<br>45 | 55<br>42 |
| Triple Jump standing start (cm) | 1<br>2 | 831<br>789 | 834<br>785 | 832<br>765 | 818<br>742 | 812<br>732 |
| Forward shot Throw (m) | 1<br>2 | 15.26<br>13.58 | 14.67<br>13.50 | 14.22<br>13.53 | 14.50<br>13.76 | 14.36<br>13.65 |

Table 1.28 – Comparison of characteristics for the best (1) and worst (2) results in female 400m sprinters in several strength, jumping, and throwing exercises.

| Exercise | | Sports Results | | | | |
|---|---|---|---|---|---|---|
| | | 50.00 – 51.00 sec | 51.00 – 52.00 sec | 52.00– 53.00 sec | 53.00 – 54.00 sec | 54.00 – 55.00 sec |
| Clean and Jerk (kg) | 1 2 | 60 40 | 60 45 | 57.5 47.5 | 52.5 40 | 52.5 40 |
| Half Squats (bar on back) (kg) | 1 2 | 115 95 | 110 90 | 100 80 | 110 85 | 95 80 |
| Broad jump standing start (cm) | 1 2 | 254 220 | 256 230 | 235 225 | 239 209 | 243 215 |
| Vertical Jump (cm) | 1 2 | 57 45 | 60 45 | 58 47 | 50 40 | 51 40 |
| Triple Jump standing start (cm) | 1 2 | 806 773 | 800 754 | 775 742 | 782 750 | 777 737 |
| Forward shot Throw (m) | 1 2 | 14.13 13.52 | 14.00 13.51 | 13.89 13.40 | 13.80 13.08 | 13.87 13.15 |

Table 1.29 – Comparison of characteristics for the best (1) and worst (2) results in female 100m hurdlers in several strength, jumping, and throwing exercises.

| Exercise | | Sports Results | | | | |
|---|---|---|---|---|---|---|
| | | 12.80 – 13.30 sec | 13.30 – 13.80 sec | 13.80– 14.30 sec | 14.30 – 14.80 sec | 14.80 – 15.30 sec |
| Clean and Jerk (kg) | 1 2 | 60 45 | 60 40 | 60 40 | 50 40 | 50 35 |
| Half Squats (bar on back) (kg) | 1 2 | 110 85 | 110 80 | 105 75 | 100 70 | 90 70 |
| Broad jumps standing start (cm) | 1 2 | 245 223 | 240 220 | 250 236 | 234 203 | 233 210 |
| Vertical Jump (cm) | 1 2 | 60 45 | 60 45 | 63 43 | 60 41 | 60 40 |
| Triple Jump standing start (cm) | 1 2 | 841 804 | 834 796 | 810 785 | 806 765 | 808 745 |
| Forward shot Throw (m) | 1 2 | 14.67 13.88 | 14.34 13.65 | 14.32 13.57 | 14.07 13.45 | 14.00 13.57 |

Table 1.30 – Comparison of characteristics for the best (1) and worst (2) results in female 400m hurdlers in several strength, jumping, and throwing exercises.

| Exercise | | Sports Results | | | | |
|---|---|---|---|---|---|---|
| | | 54.00 – 55.00 sec | 55.00 – 56.00 sec | 56.00– 57.00 sec | 57.00 – 58.00 sec | 58.00 – 59.00 sec |
| Clean and Jerk (kg) | 1 | 55 | 55 | 50 | 50 | 45 |
| | 2 | 60 | 62.5 | 57.5 | 55 | 50 |
| Half Squats (bar on back) (kg) | 1 | 100 | 100 | 100 | 90 | 90 |
| | 2 | 80 | 85 | 80 | 70 | 70 |
| Broad jump standing start (cm) | 1 | 254 | 243 | 232 | 237 | 235 |
| | 2 | 235 | 220 | 209 | 203 | 212 |
| Vertical Jump (cm) | 1 | 60 | 63 | 60 | 56 | 55 |
| | 2 | 49 | 50 | 47 | 45 | 43 |
| Triple Jump standing start (cm) | 1 | 834 | 823 | 818 | 834 | 798 |
| | 2 | 797 | 790 | 781 | 765 | 753 |
| Forward shot Throw (m) | 1 | 14.75 | 14.23 | 14.44 | 14.07 | 14.01 |
| | 2 | 14.12 | 13.76 | 13.87 | 13.43 | 14.50 |

# Chapter 2: Transfer of Training in the Jumping Events

In the training of jumpers a large number of exercises are used that help to improve several critical, physical qualities. Specifically, we are talking about the development of maximal speed and special strength. If the development of maximal speed occurs as a result of using various running (short sprints) and jumping exercises (standing jumps, repeated jumps, etc.) then accomplishing the task of developing special strength occurs due to the use of various speed and throwing exercises. In this chapter, we intend to identify the positive transfer between various types of exercises and their analogues that are most often used in athletes of various sports qualification during the training process. In the given experimental material (Tables 2.1 – 2.8) we will compare indicators of various types of running (sprints), strength, and other exercises with the results of athletes in competition exercises.

Table 2.1 shows the correlation coefficients between results in competition exercises and several running (sprinting), strength, jumping, and throwing exercises. The greatest transfer was seen between the indicators for the 60m sprint from blocks, a broad jump from a short approach, and in ten-fold jumps from a standing start. In the first case the correlation coefficient fluctuated between 0.732 - 0.834, in the second: from 0.705 – 0.887, and in the third: from 0.720 – 0803. Indicators of transfer in other exercises, besides the snatch and backward shot throw, were significantly lower (especially in the half squat). On all levels of sports mastery a correlation existed between competition results and the results in the snatch and the backward shot throw.

Table 2.1 – Correlational relationship between competition results for male long jumpers and various developmental exercises.

| No. | Exercise | Sports Result / Coefficient Correlation | | | | |
|---|---|---|---|---|---|---|
| | | 8.20 – 7.90 meters | 7.90 – 7.60 meters | 7.60 – 7.30 meters | 7.30 – 7.00 meters | 7.00 – 6.50 meters |
| 1 | 30m sprint run start | 0.785 | 0.706 | 0.734 | 0.712 | 0.703 |
| 2 | 30m sprint from blocks | 0.689 | 0.734 | 0.676 | 0.715 | 0.744 |
| 3 | 60m sprint from blocks | 0.806 | 0.834 | 0.745 | 0.756 | 0.732 |
| 4 | 100m sprint from blocks | 0.680 | 0.735 | 0.765 | 0.704 | 0.706 |
| 5 | Broad jump standing start | 0.708 | 0.734 | 0.705 | 0.652 | 0.634 |
| 6 | Triple jump | 0.711 | 0.698 | 0.731 | 0.706 | 0.700 |
| 7 | 5 fold jumps standing start | 0.756 | 0.723 | 0.711 | 0.687 | 0.692 |
| 8 | 10 fold jumps standing start | 0.803 | 0.786 | 0.765 | 0.777 | 0.720 |
| 9 | Long jump run start | 0.887 | 0.865 | 0.807 | 0.798 | 0.750 |
| 10 | Snatch | 0.308 | 0.345 | 0.333 | 0.306 | 0.324 |
| 11 | Half Squat | 0.402 | 0.396 | 0.405 | 0.432 | 0.409 |
| 12 | Backward shot throw | 0.245 | 0.206 | 0.200 | 0.270 | 0.267 |

In Table 2.2, correlational analyses for high jumpers are shown. Here, in most cases, the correlational relationship was lower than in that of the broad jumpers. This occurred in three running exercises and in all jumping exercises with a standing start. All levels of sports mastery showed positive transfer with competition exercises. The greatest correlation was observed between the results in the high jump and the short sprints (0.907, 0.932, 0.915, 0.898, and 0.906), between the broad jump with a full approach (0.898, 0.944, 0.904, 0.924, and 0.906), and the squat (0.766, 0.712, 0.734, 0.707, and 0.700). On all levels of sports mastery there was not one case where a correlation was observed between the snatch or backward shot throw and results in the competition exercise. Several other indicators of positive transfer between competition exercises and other exercises were observed in the triple jump with a short approach (0.956, 0.921, 0.905, 0.922, and 0.898), in the ten-fold jumps from a standing start (0.934, 0.901, 0.920, 0.903, and 0.912), and five-fold jumps from a standing start (0.912, 0.898, 0.932, 0.800, and 0.856). In comparison with indicators for long jumpers, indicators for high jumpers were significantly higher in the squat. Here is the comparison: 0.402 to 0.766, 0.396 to 0.712, 0.405 to 0.734, 0.432 to 0.707, 0.409 to 0.700). We also observe a very slight positive transfer in the snatch and the backward shot throw (see Table 2.3).

Table 2.2 – Correlational relationship between competition results for male high jumpers and various developmental exercises.

| No. | Exercise | Sports Result / Coefficient Correlation | | | | |
|---|---|---|---|---|---|---|
| | | 8.20 – 7.90 meters | 7.90 – 7.60 meters | 7.60 – 7.30 meters | 7.30 – 7.00 meters | 7.00 – 6.50 meters |
| 1 | 30m sprint run start | 0.405 | 0.432 | 0.423 | 0.400 | 0.398 |
| 2 | 30m sprint from blocks | 0.412 | 0.444 | 0.397 | 0.408 | 0.467 |
| 3 | 60m sprint from blocks | 0.500 | 0.432 | 0.427 | 0.395 | 0.456 |
| 4 | 100m sprint from blocks | 0.709 | 0.711 | 0.678 | 0.657 | 0.634 |
| 5 | Broad jump standing start | 0.645 | 0.607 | 0.612 | 0.576 | 0.544 |
| 6 | Triple jump | 0.465 | 0.505 | 0.564 | 0.576 | 0.457 |
| 7 | 5 fold jumps standing start | 0.623 | 0.670 | 0.602 | 0.587 | 0.555 |
| 8 | 10 fold jumps standing start | 0.898 | 0.944 | 0.904 | 0.924 | 0.906 |
| 9 | Long jump run start | 0.907 | 0.932 | 0.915 | 0.898 | 0.906 |
| 10 | Snatch | 0.234 | 0.336 | 0.367 | 0.365 | 0.298 |
| 11 | Half Squat | 0.766 | 0.712 | 0.734 | 0.707 | 0.700 |
| 12 | Backward Shot throw | 0.200 | 0.306 | 0.321 | 0.305 | 0.320 |

Table 2.3 – Correlational relationship between competition results for male triple jumpers and various developmental exercises.

| No. | Exercise | Sports Result / Coefficient Correlation | | | | |
|---|---|---|---|---|---|---|
| | | 17.00 – 16.50 meters | 16.50 – 16.00 meters | 16.00 – 15.50 meters | 15.50 – 15.00 meters | 15.00 – 14.00 meters |
| 1 | 30m sprint run start | 0.766 | 0.805 | 0.734 | 0.770 | 0.785 |
| 2 | 30m sprint from blocks | 0.710 | 0.798 | 0.756 | 0.790 | 0.765 |
| 3 | 60m sprint from blocks | 0.825 | 0.804 | 0.768 | 0.786 | 0.705 |
| 4 | 100m sprint from blocks | 0.789 | 0.788 | 0.706 | 0.755 | 0.734 |
| 5 | Broad jump standing start | 0.809 | 0.734 | 0.700 | 0.705 | 0.687 |
| 6 | Triple jump | 0.834 | 0.800 | 0.812 | 0.765 | 0.707 |
| 7 | 5 fold jumps standing start | 0.912 | 0.898 | 0.932 | 0.800 | 0.856 |
| 8 | 10 fold jumps standing start | 0.934 | 0.901 | 0.920 | 0.903 | 0.912 |
| 9 | Long jump run start | 0.956 | 0.921 | 0.906 | 0.922 | 0.898 |
| 10 | Snatch | 0.345 | 0.304 | 0.289 | 0.297 | 0.326 |
| 11 | Half Squat | 0.500 | 0.465 | 0.488 | 0.432 | 0.398 |
| 12 | Backward shot throw | 0.201 | 0.323 | 0.190 | 0.306 | 0.297 |

Table 2.4 shows the indicators of correlational analysis for pole vaulters. The highest correlation for this group existed between competition exercises and the vault with a short approach (0.924, 0.907, 0.890, 0.921 and 0.887), in a 30m sprint with buildup (0.807, 0.819, .0.890, 0 865, and 0.805), in a 30m sprint from blocks (0.788, 0.800, 0.776, 0.765, 0.778), and in a 60m sprint from blocks (0.812, 0.834, 0.796, 0.805, 0.767). In all other exercises, positive transfer was observed on all levels of sports mastery, from 4m to 5m.

Table 2.4 – Correlational relationship between competition results for male pole vaulters and various developmental exercises.

| No. | Exercise | Sports Result / Coefficient Correlation | | | | |
|---|---|---|---|---|---|---|
| | | 5.80 – 5.50 meters | 5.50 – 5.20 meters | 5.20 – 4.90 meters | 4.90 – 4.60 meters | 4.60 – 4.00 meters |
| 1 | 30m sprint run start | 0.807 | 0.819 | 0.890 | 0.805 | 0.805 |
| 2 | 30m sprint from blocks | 0.788 | 0.800 | 0.776 | 0.765 | 0.779 |
| 3 | 60m sprint from blocks | 0.812 | 0.834 | 0.796 | 0.805 | 0.767 |
| 4 | 100m sprint from blocks | 0.706 | 0.765 | 0.712 | 0.756 | 0.709 |
| 5 | Broad jump standing start | 0.606 | 0.598 | 0.634 | 0.635 | 0.590 |
| 6 | Vertical jump | 0.665 | 0.706 | 0.687 | 0.609 | 0.624 |
| 7 | 5 fold jumps standing start | 0.600 | 0.607 | 0.576 | 0.543 | 0.599 |
| 8 | Triple jump | 0.678 | 0.615 | 0.588 | 0.635 | 0.612 |
| 9 | Pole Vault short approach | 0.924 | 0.907 | 0.890 | 0.921 | 0.887 |
| 10 | Snatch | 0.390 | 0.405 | 0.430 | 0.400 | 0.396 |
| 11 | Half Squat | 0.437 | 0.409 | 0.556 | 0.500 | 0.476 |
| 12 | Bench Press | 0.390 | 0.423 | 0.405 | 0.436 | 0.403 |
| 13 | Long Jump run start | 0.745 | 0.723 | 0.700 | 0.687 | 0.668 |

Analysis of the data presented in Tables 2.5 – 2.8 highlights the fact that, according to the data gathered and presented in these books, a correlational relationship exists between competition and assistance type exercises in every type of jumps. Moreover, it shows that the results in competition exercises are greater in this current day of sport than they were in the previous years (1980-2000). Indeed, female long jumpers in two cases, achieved higher transfer in tenfold jumps with a standing start and long jump with a short approach. Here the difference in correlational relationship was as follows: tenfold jumps - 0.832, 0.800, 0.765, 0.723, 0.708 and correspondingly – 0.780, 0.804, 0.757, 0.700, 0.699; long jump with a short approach – 0.924, 0.956, 0.914, 0.903, 0.913 and correspondingly - 0.924, 0.967, 0.876, 0.803, 0.856. In the first column of numbers indicators of correlational relationships in athletes from the year 2000 and later are displayed and the second – athletes from before the year 2000. Only slightly did the indicators change for the 30m sprint with a short approach - 0.823, 0.809, 0.854, 0.814, 0.812 and correspondingly – 0.876, 0.824, 0.855, 0.789, 0.824. We see a similar trend among high jumpers as well. Again, the most telling indicators were results in the high jump with a short approach and the long jump with a full approach. Indicators of correlational analysis between competition results and results in the long jump with a full approach and in the high jump with a short approach were as follows: 0.832, 0.800, 0.777, 0.798, 0.765 and correspondingly – 0.778, 0.765, 0.680, 0.724, 0.808, in the high jump with a short approach – 0.923, 0.944, 0.905, 0.898, 0.906 and correspondingly – 0.886, 0.965, 0.905, 0.890, 0.865. This tendency is observed in triple jumpers as well. In this type of jumps, the most telling indicators were the triple jump with a short approach and the tenfold jumps from a standing start. When compared with results in athletes from the previous century, it becomes clear that positive transfer between these exercises has been observed more in athletes of the current century. Here we will look at the following indicators: triple jump with a short approach - 0.943, 0.907, 0.878, 0.856, 0.874 compared to 0.906, 0.866, 0.776, 0.754, 0.700, and in a tenfold jump – 0.900, 0.912, 0.876, 0.853, 0.897 and correspondingly – 0.865, 0.886, 0.854, 0.786, 0790.

In athletes specializing in the long jump, high jump, and triple jump, there is no positive transfer of training observed in the backward shot throw. That being said, transfer exists for athletes on all levels of sports mastery in all running, as well as jumping exercises from a standing start. In closing, I point out that between results in competition exercises and in the squat, there was a positive transfer on all levels of sports mastery. For the snatch and the long jump, transfer was only observed on the three highest levels of sports mastery. Pole vaulters of all qualification levels demonstrated transfer while no transfer was observed for triple and high jumpers.

Table 2.5 – Correlational relationship between competition results for female long jumpers and various developmental exercises.

| No. | Exercise | Sports Result / Coefficient Correlation | | | | |
|---|---|---|---|---|---|---|
| | | 7.00 – 6.70 meters | 6.70 – 6.40 meters | 6.40 – 6.10 meters | 6.10 – 5.50 meters | 5.50 – 5.00 meters |
| 1 | 30m sprint run start | 0.823 | 0.809 | 0.854 | 0.814 | 0.812 |
| 2 | 30m sprint from blocks | 0.754 | 0.780 | 0.731 | 0.756 | 0.704 |
| 3 | 60m sprint from blocks | 0.799 | 0.817 | 0.734 | 0.788 | 0.805 |
| 4 | 100m sprint from blocks | 0.723 | 0.700 | 0.721 | 0.698 | 0.745 |
| 5 | Broad jump standing start | 0.675 | 0.620 | 0.653 | 0.700 | 0.637 |
| 6 | Triple jump | 0.707 | 0.654 | 0.623 | 0.678 | 0.619 |
| 7 | 5 fold jumps standing start | 0.709 | 0.698 | 0.734 | 0.686 | 0.700 |
| 8 | 10 fold jumps standing start | 0.832 | 0.800 | 0.765 | 0.732 | 0.708 |
| 9 | Long jump run start | 0.924 | 0.956 | 0.914 | 0.903 | 0.913 |
| 10 | Snatch | 0.356 | 0.345 | 0.395 | 0.400 | 0.405 |
| 11 | Half Squat | 0.409 | 0.523 | 0.466 | 0.506 | 0.465 |
| 12 | Backward shot throw | 0.200 | 0.256 | 0.312 | 0.275 | 0.233 |

Table 2.6 – Correlational relationship between competition results for female high jumpers and various developmental exercises.

| No. | Exercise | Sports Result / Coefficient Correlation | | | | |
|---|---|---|---|---|---|---|
| | | 2.00 – 1.90 meters | 1.90 – 1.80 meters | 1.80 – 1.70 meters | 1.70 – 1.60 meters | 1.60 – 1.50 meters |
| 1 | 30m sprint run start | 0.578 | 0.600 | 0.732 | 0.687 | 0.650 |
| 2 | 30m sprint from blocks | 0.488 | 0.507 | 0.534 | 0.566 | 0.508 |
| 3 | 60m sprint from blocks | 0.434 | 0.500 | 0.487 | 0.431 | 0.465 |
| 4 | 100m sprint from blocks | 0.643 | 0.654 | 0.503 | 0.678 | 0.600 |
| 5 | Broad jump standing start | 0.609 | 0.675 | 0.615 | 0.675 | 0.612 |
| 6 | Triple jump | 0.587 | 0.653 | 0.600 | 0.703 | 0.634 |
| 7 | 5 fold jumps standing start | 0.700 | 0.653 | 0.632 | 0.675 | 0.598 |
| 8 | 10 fold jumps standing start | 0.832 | 0.800 | 0.777 | 0.798 | 0.765 |
| 9 | Long jump run start | 0.923 | 0.944 | 0.905 | 0.898 | 0.906 |
| 10 | Snatch | 0.234 | 0.270 | 0.255 | 0.312 | 0.290 |
| 11 | Half Squat | 0.724 | 0.688 | 0.709 | 0.722 | 0.705 |
| 12 | Backward shot throw | 0.212 | 0.255 | 0.305 | 0.356 | 0.307 |

Table 2.7 – Correlational relationship between competition results for female triple jumpers and various developmental exercises.

| No. | Exercise | Sports Result / Coefficient Correlation | | | | |
|---|---|---|---|---|---|---|
| | | 14.50 – 14.00 meters | 14.00 – 13.50 meters | 13.50 – 13.00 meters | 13.00 – 12.50 meters | 12.50 – 12.00 meters |
| 1 | 30m sprint run start | 0.813 | 0.832 | 0.790 | 0.800 | 0.776 |
| 2 | 30m sprint from blocks | 0.778 | 0.800 | 0.767 | 0.785 | 0.800 |
| 3 | 60m sprint from blocks | 0.800 | 0.786 | 0.778 | 0.797 | 0.786 |
| 4 | 100m sprint from blocks | 0.765 | 0.669 | 0.702 | 0.705 | 0.698 |
| 5 | Broad jump standing start | 0.706 | 0.675 | 0.608 | 0.642 | 0.597 |
| 6 | Triple jump | 0.807 | 0.765 | 0.644 | 0.645 | 0.578 |
| 7 | 5 fold jumps standing start | 0.834 | 0.809 | 0.824 | 0.797 | 0.812 |
| 8 | 10 fold jumps standing start | 0.900 | 0.912 | 0.876 | 0.853 | 0.897 |
| 9 | Long jump run start | 0.943 | 0.907 | 0.878 | 0.856 | 0.874 |
| 10 | Snatch | 0.306 | 0.324 | 0.354 | 0.300 | 0.298 |
| 11 | Half Squat | 0.654 | 0.675 | 0.573 | 0.588 | 0.543 |
| 12 | Backward shot throw | 0.267 | 0.250 | 0.307 | 0.300 | 0.287 |

Table 2.8 – Correlational relationship between competition results for female pole vaulters and various developmental exercises.

| No. | Exercise | Sports Result / Coefficient Correlation | | | | |
|---|---|---|---|---|---|---|
| | | 4.50 – 4.20 meters | 4.20 – 3.90 meters | 3.90 – 3.60 meters | 3.60 – 3.30 meters | 3.30 – 3.00 meters |
| 1 | 30m sprint run start | 0.789 | 0.812 | 0.800 | 0.788 | 0.765 |
| 2 | 30m sprint from blocks | 0.777 | 0.798 | 0.767 | 0.789 | 0.745 |
| 3 | 60m sprint from blocks | 0.805 | 0.743 | 0.756 | 0.708 | 0.676 |
| 4 | 100m sprint from blocks | 0.789 | 0.765 | 0.743 | 0.690 | 0.666 |
| 5 | Broad jump standing start | 0.775 | 0.723 | 0.708 | 0.734 | 0.676 |
| 6 | Vertical jump | 0.666 | 0.696 | 0.708 | 0.705 | 0.643 |
| 7 | 5 fold jumps standing start | 0.650 | 0.700 | 0.603 | 0.634 | 0.600 |
| 8 | Triple jump | 0.634 | 0.654 | 0.600 | 0.589 | 0.607 |
| 9 | Pole Vault short approach | 0.900 | 0.876 | 0.877 | 0.895 | 0.786 |
| 10 | Snatch | 0.444 | 0.527 | 0.497 | 0.421 | 0.432 |
| 11 | Half Squat | 0.489 | 0.453 | 0.510 | 0.564 | 0.476 |
| 12 | Bench Press | 0.507 | 0.498 | 0.517 | 0.487 | 0.400 |
| 13 | Backward shot throw | 0.778 | 0.705 | 0.765 | 0.708 | 0.766 |

In Table 2.9, experimental data is presented that shows the best and worst results in several strength, jumping, and throwing exercises on five levels of sports mastery – from 6.00m to 8.20m. Notice the fact that in all types of exercises we see a general trend – in the overwhelming majority of cases a decrease in sports results for male long jumpers is shown by a decrease in the best and worst results in indicator lifts as well. The greatest difference was between the half squat – 40kg, the standing broad jump – 35cm, and in the triple jump from a standing start – 47cm. In athletes specializing in the high jump, there was a similar general trend of decreasing indicators for the best and worst numbers in the test exercises as sports mastery decreased (Table 2.10). The greatest difference between the best and worst result was between the two strength exercises (snatch – 17.5 and half squat – 40kg), in the broad jump from a standing start – 28cm, and in the triple jump – 22cm. It follows to note that the smallest difference between the various test exercises on all levels of sports mastery was observed in the snatch (at the level of 2.30 – 2.20cm, 80kg and at the level of 1.80 – 1.70cm, 75kg).

Table 2.9 – Comparison of characteristics for the best (1) and worst (2) results in male long jumpers in several strength, jumping, and throwing exercises.

| Exercise | | Sports Result | | | | |
|---|---|---|---|---|---|---|
| | | 8.20 – 7.90m | 7.90 – 7.60m | 7.60 – 7.30m | 7.30 – 6.50m | 6.50 – 6.00m |
| Snatch (kg) | 1 | 87.5 | 85 | 85 | 82.5 | 80 |
| | 2 | 70 | 67.5 | 75 | 70 | 65 |
| Half Squat (kg) | 1 | 190 | 185 | 180 | 175 | 175 |
| | 2 | 155 | 155 | 140 | 145 | 140 |
| Broad Jump (cm) | 1 | 343 | 341 | 327 | 319 | 313 |
| | 2 | 312 | 306 | 307 | 302 | 299 |
| Vertical Jump (cm) | 1 | 85 | 87 | 83 | 85 | 78 |
| | 2 | 75 | 75 | 70 | 75 | 67 |
| Triple Jump (cm) | 1 | 944 | 923 | 919 | 921 | 906 |
| | 2 | 897 | 889 | 900 | 895 | 876 |
| Backward shot Throw (m) | 1 | 16.35 | 16.47 | 15.77 | 16.00 | 15.75 |
| | 2 | 15.67 | 15.96 | 15.34 | 15.66 | 15.09 |

Table 2.10 – Comparison of characteristics for the best (1) and worst (2) results in male high jumpers in several strength, jumping, and throwing exercises.

| Exercise | | Sports Result | | | | |
|---|---|---|---|---|---|---|
| | | 2.30 – 2.20m | 2.20 – 2.10m | 2.10 – 2.00m | 2.00 – 1.90m | 1.90 – 1.80m |
| Snatch (kg) | 1 | 80 | 77.5 | 75 | 70 | 75 |
| | 2 | 65 | 60 | 62.5 | 60 | 60 |
| Half Squat (kg) | 1 | 195 | 185 | 175 | 165 | 150 |
| | 2 | 165 | 165 | 135 | 135 | 130 |
| Broad Jump (cm) | 1 | 334 | 325 | 320 | 317 | 313 |
| | 2 | 306 | 307 | 296 | 290 | 291 |
| Vertical Jump (cm) | 1 | 85 | 86 | 83 | 78 | 75 |
| | 2 | 73 | 77 | 74 | 69 | 66 |
| Triple Jump (cm) | 1 | 932 | 922 | 916 | 907 | 902 |
| | 2 | 915 | 907 | 896 | 888 | 880 |
| Backward shot Throw (m) | 1 | 16.45 | 16.30 | 15.87 | 16.00 | 15.50 |
| | 2 | 15.66 | 15.60 | 15.45 | 15.43 | 14.93 |

Table 2.11 shows the difference between the best and worst results in test exercises for all levels of sports mastery in triple jumpers. Here we observe the same tendency of decreasing results according the level of sports mastery of the athletes. The greatest difference between the best and worst indicators was observed between the following exercises: snatch – 12.5kg (17-16.50m level), half squat – 45kg (16.50 – 16.00m level), broad

jump from a standing start – 27m (17.00 – 16.50m level), vertical jump – 15cm (17.00 – 16.50 level), and the triple jump from a standing start – 79cm (17.99 – 16.50m level).

Table 2.11 – Comparison of characteristics for the best (1) and worst (2) results in male triple jumpers in several strength, jumping, and throwing exercises.

| Exercise | | Sports Result | | | | |
|---|---|---|---|---|---|---|
| | | 17.00 – 16.50m | 16.50 – 16.00m | 16.00 – 15.50m | 15.50 – 15.00m | 15.00 – 14.00m |
| Snatch (kg) | 1 | 85 | 75 | 77.5 | 70 | 67.5 |
| | 2 | 67.5 | 65 | 65 | 60 | 60 |
| Half Squat (kg) | 1 | 180 | 180 | 170 | 170 | 160 |
| | 2 | 140 | 135 | 135 | 130 | 125 |
| Broad Jump (cm) | 1 | 333 | 320 | 315 | 320 | 310 |
| | 2 | 306 | 305 | 300 | 298 | 297 |
| Vertical Jump (cm) | 1 | 80 | 70 | 73 | 75 | 70 |
| | 2 | 65 | 60 | 66 | 65 | 58 |
| Triple Jump (cm) | 1 | 988 | 956 | 945 | 932 | 927 |
| | 2 | 909 | 911 | 921 | 914 | 900 |
| Backward shot Throw (m) | 1 | 15.78 | 16.32 | 16.00 | 15.89 | 15.76 |
| | 2 | 15.43 | 15.75 | 15.23 | 15.33 | 15.21 |

Table 2.12 shows the difference between the best and worst indicators for pole vaulters. They are slightly different from the results shown in triple jumpers. In the snatch, the best results differed by 15kg between the 5.80m – 5.50m groups, and in the 4.6 – 4.0 m group, the half squat differed by 30kg. In the standing broad jump the difference was 28cm for the 4.60 – 4.00m level and in the standing triple jump – 35cm (in the 5.80 – 5.30m level).

If we analyze the general tendency of decrease in the best and worst results in the given jumping events (Tables 2.9 – 2.13) according to the decrease in sports results on each respective level of sports mastery, the backward shot throw decreases as sports mastery decreases in the overwhelming majority of cases (24 compared to 4 in other jumps).

Table 2.12 – Comparison of characteristics for the best (1) and worst (2) results in male pole vaulters in several strength, jumping, and throwing exercises.

| Exercise | | Sports Result | | | | |
|---|---|---|---|---|---|---|
| | | 5.80 – 5.50m | 5.50 – 5.20m | 5.20 – 4.90m | 4.90 – 4.60m | 4.60 – 4.00m |
| Snatch (kg) | 1 | 90 | 85 | 80 | 80 | 75 |
| | 2 | 70 | 75 | 67.5 | 70 | 62.5 |
| Half Squat (kg) | 1 | 180 | 175 | 175 | 165 | 160 |
| | 2 | 150 | 150 | 140 | 140 | 130 |
| Broad Jump (cm) | 1 | 326 | 324 | 317 | 318 | 315 |
| | 2 | 300 | 309 | 303 | 295 | 287 |
| Vertical Jump (cm) | 1 | 83 | 80 | 82 | 77 | 70 |
| | 2 | 65 | 66 | 62 | 68 | 62 |
| Triple Jump (cm) | 1 | 925 | 917 | 909 | 900 | 889 |
| | 2 | 890 | 895 | 885 | 876 | 865 |
| Backward shot Throw (m) | 1 | 16.34 | 15.87 | 15.66 | 15.89 | 15.43 |
| | 2 | 15.76 | 15.08 | 14.90 | 15.43 | 14.86 |

Table 2.13 shows the best and worst results for athletes specializing in the long jump. In most of the test exercises, no trend was observed in decreasing results according to sports mastery. Rather, the best and worst results were similar for athletes regardless of sports mastery. In the snatch, the best result (65kg) was shown in athletes of two different levels of qualification (7.00 – 6.70m, 6.40 – 6.10m), and the worst (40kg) – on three levels (6.40-6.10m, 6.10 - 5.50m and 5.50 - 5.00m). In the half squat, the best result (135kg) was achieved by athletes in the 6.40 – 6.70m group and the worst (90kg) – in the 5.0 – 5.50m. group. In the standing broad jump, the difference between the best (7.00 – 6.70m level) and worst (6.10 – 5.50 level) was 16cm (6.40 – 6.70m. group), as well as in the vertical jump. In the triple jump from a standing start, there was a tendency for the results to decrease according to sports mastery: 836, 830, 825, 819, and 809cm. The difference between the best and worst indicators was 48cm (in the 6.50 – 6.10m group). The best result in the backward shot throw (15.56m) was in the 6.10 – 5.50m group and the worst result was in the 6.40 – 6.10m. group. A few other tendencies between the best and worst results were observed in the high jumpers (Table 2.14). In three test exercises (snatch, half squat, and standing broad jump) sports results got worse according to decreasing sports qualification and in three other exercises (vertical jump, standing start triple jump, shot throw backward), we see the opposite trend. For example, here are the best and worst results in the backward shot throw: 15.00, 14.87, 15.45, 14.90, and 14.76.

Table 2.13 – Comparison of characteristics for the best (1) and worst (2) results in female long jumpers in several strength, jumping, and throwing exercises.

| Exercise | | Sports Result | | | | |
|---|---|---|---|---|---|---|
| | | 7.00 – 6.70m | 6.70 – 6.40m | 6.40 – 6.10m | 6.10 – 5.50m | 5.50 – 5.00m |
| Snatch (kg) | 1 | 65 | 60 | 65 | 50 | 50 |
| | 2 | 45 | 50 | 40 | 40 | 40 |
| Half Squat (kg) | 1 | 130 | 135 | 125 | 120 | 120 |
| | 2 | 115 | 120 | 115 | 100 | 90 |
| Broad Jump (cm) | 1 | 270 | 265 | 260 | 263 | 260 |
| | 2 | 254 | 249 | 245 | 240 | 246 |
| Vertical Jump (cm) | 1 | 66 | 65 | 62 | 59 | 55 |
| | 2 | 51 | 49 | 50 | 44 | 45 |
| Triple Jump (cm) | 1 | 836 | 830 | 825 | 819 | 809 |
| | 2 | 800 | 821 | 777 | 782 | 780 |
| Backward shot Throw (m) | 1 | 15.32 | 15.20 | 14.88 | 15.56 | 15.13 |
| | 2 | 14.56 | 14.69 | 14.23 | 14.35 | 14.76 |

Table 2.14 – Comparison of characteristics for the best (1) and worst (2) results in female high jumpers in several strength, jumping, and throwing exercises.

| Exercise | | Sports Result | | | | |
|---|---|---|---|---|---|---|
| | | 2.00 – 1.90m | 1.90 – 1.80m | 1.80 – 1.70m | 1.70 – 1.60m | 1.60 – 1.50m |
| Snatch (kg) | 1 | 60 | 60 | 55 | 50 | 50 |
| | 2 | 45 | 42.5 | 47.5 | 40 | 40 |
| Half Squat (kg) | 1 | 145 | 140 | 135 | 125 | 110 |
| | 2 | 110 | 110 | 100 | 100 | 90 |
| Broad Jump (cm) | 1 | 270 | 260 | 253 | 248 | 240 |
| | 2 | 250 | 240 | 240 | 230 | 221 |
| Vertical Jump (cm) | 1 | 70 | 65 | 67 | 63 | 55 |
| | 2 | 57 | 50 | 49 | 50 | 46 |
| Triple Jump (cm) | 1 | 822 | 809 | 819 | 806 | 800 |
| | 2 | 786 | 775 | 761 | 770 | 765 |
| Backward shot Throw (m) | 1 | 15.00 | 14.87 | 15.45 | 14.90 | 14.76 |
| | 2 | 14.56 | 14.50 | 14.75 | 14.45 | 14.32 |

Table 2.15 shows the dynamics of the best and worst results on all levels of sports mastery for triple jumpers. Only in two exercises was a decrease in the best result observed according to a decreasing level of sports mastery: the squat and the standing start triple jump. If the difference between the best and worst results in the snatch was 15kg, which happened frequently for this exercise, then in the squat, it rose above 35kg (at the level of 12.50 – 12.00m). In the long jump, the best result was 2.67m (at the level of 14.50 – 14.00m),

and the worst – 2.02m (at the level of 13.00 – 12.50m). The difference between the best and worst results in the vertical jump was 17cm. This was significant compared to other exercises, that is, if we look at the results from a percentage change perspective. The best result in the three fold jumps from a standing start was 8.37m, and the worst – 1.45m. The dynamics of the best and worst results in the backward shot throw show a wavelike pattern. For example, the dynamics of best and worst results from one level of sports mastery were as follows: 14.89, 15.00, 14.76, 14.88, and 14.79m.

Table 2.15 – Comparison of characteristics for the best (1) and worst (2) results in female triple jumpers in several strength, jumping, and throwing exercises.

| Exercise | | Sports Result | | | | |
|---|---|---|---|---|---|---|
| | | 14.50 – 14.00m | 14.00 – 13.50m | 13.50 – 13.00m | 13.00 – 12.50m | 12.50 – 12.00m |
| Snatch (kg) | 1 | 60 | 65 | 60 | 55 | 55 |
| | 2 | 45 | 45 | 47.5 | 40 | 42.5 |
| Half Squat (kg) | 1 | 125 | 120 | 120 | 120 | 115 |
| | 2 | 100 | 90 | 85 | 90 | 80 |
| Broad Jump (cm) | 1 | 267 | 253 | 246 | 230 | 238 |
| | 2 | 239 | 240 | 231 | 202 | 216 |
| Vertical Jump (cm) | 1 | 67 | 62 | 56 | 59 | 50 |
| | 2 | 50 | 55 | 43 | 42 | 40 |
| Triple Jump (cm) | 1 | 837 | 820 | 809 | 795 | 786 |
| | 2 | 792 | 795 | 766 | 765 | 745 |
| Backward shot Throw (m) | 1 | 14.89 | 15.00 | 14.76 | 14.88 | 14.79 |
| | 2 | 14.45 | 14.30 | 14.23 | 14.21 | 14.34 |

Table 2.16 shows the dynamics of best and worst results in athletes specializing in the pole vault. In all exercises, a wavelike pattern was observed in the changes among test exercise results across all levels of sports mastery. For example, in the snatch the best result followed the next best in the following manner - 67.5kg (4.50-4.20m level), 62.50kg (4.20 - 3.90m level), 65kg (level 3.90-3.60m), 55kg (3.60-3.30m level), 50kg (3.30-3.00m level). The difference between the best and worst results reached 17kg. There was not a larger difference between the best and worst results in the squat than 35kg; that is, if we look not only at the weight, but at the percent change. The best result in the standing broad jump (2.43m) was in the 3.90 – 3.30 group and the worst (2.10m) was in the 4.20 – 3.90m group. The best and the worst results were similar at the 4.50 – 4.30m level – 67cm and 45cm. There was a less significant change in the best and worst results for the three fold jumps from a standing start and the backward shot throw.

Table 2.16 – Comparison of characteristics for the best (1) and worst (2) results in female pole vaulters in several strength, jumping, and throwing exercises.

| Exercise | | Sports Result | | | | |
|---|---|---|---|---|---|---|
| | | 4.50 – 4.20m | 4.20 – 3.90m | 3.90 – 3.60m | 3.60 – 3.30m | 3.30 – 3.00m |
| Snatch (kg) | 1 | 67.5 | 62.5 | 65 | 55 | 50 |
| | 2 | 50 | 45 | 50 | 40 | 37.5 |
| Half Squat (kg) | 1 | 120 | 120 | 110 | 110 | 100 |
| | 2 | 80 | 85 | 75 | 70 | 70 |
| Broad Jump (cm) | 1 | 240 | 235 | 243 | 230 | 227 |
| | 2 | 220 | 210 | 219 | 218 | 209 |
| Vertical Jump (cm) | 1 | 67 | 65 | 65 | 67 | 65 |
| | 2 | 45 | 55 | 50 | 45 | 51 |
| Triple Jump (cm) | 1 | 830 | 819 | 811 | 800 | 803 |
| | 2 | 800 | 793 | 788 | 770 | 767 |
| Backward shot Throw (m) | 1 | 15.24 | 14.67 | 15.03 | 14.89 | 14.78 |
| | 2 | 14.80 | 13.87 | 14.53 | 14.37 | 14.10 |

# Chapter 3: Transfer of Training in the Throws

In the process of training athletes of various sports qualification who specialize in the throws, many different types of throwing, strength, running, jumping, and other exercises are used. In some cases, these exercises are similar to each other in many parameters (for example, biomechanical similarities) and in other cases they are not. Despite these differences, many specialists are of the opinion that positive correlations exist between them. For this, they use various test exercises that can demonstrate the nature of these correlations. We will also talk about this practice when we address the problem of training transfer in each type of respective throw.

Table 3.1 shows the dynamics of the correlational relationships for male shot putters of various sports qualifications between the competition weight shot and lighter or heavier shot weights. In the shot throw with 5kg and 6kg, there is a tendency for the results to consistently decrease according to higher and higher levels of sports mastery. In the shot throw of 8, 9, and 10kg, we see the opposite dynamic – according to better levels of sports mastery, results were better and better. For example, in the 14-15m shot throw level (8kg shot) the correlation coefficient was 0.688 and at the 21-22m level it was 0.956. There is also an interesting correlation between the shot throw with a 6kg implement where the relationship was approximately equal among all levels of sports mastery.

Table 3.1 – Correlation comparison between indicators of preparedness in male shot putters along with results for competition, lighter and heavier implements. For levels 1-3, heavier implements were not used as their level of sports mastery did not warrant this means of training.

| Number | Exercise | Sports Result (m), coefficient correlation | | | | | | |
|---|---|---|---|---|---|---|---|---|
| | | 14-15 | 15-16 | 16-17 | 17-18 | 18-19 | 19-20 | 21-22 |
| 1 | Shot Put 5kg | 0.807 | 0.743 | 0.732 | 0.744 | 0.708 | 0.706 | 0.654 |
| 2 | Shot Put 6kg | 0.776 | 0.780 | 0.756 | 0.687 | 0.654 | 0.650 | 0.614 |
| 3 | Shot Put 8kg | 0.688 | 0.675 | 0.798 | 0.806 | 0.856 | 0.887 | 0.956 |
| 4 | Shot Put 9kg | - | - | 0.665 | 0.786 | 0.806 | 0.900 | 0.934 |
| 5 | Shot Put 10kg | - | - | - | 0.634 | 0.786 | 0.897 | 0.925 |
| 6 | Standing Shot put 6kg | 0.800 | 0.867 | 0.886 | 0.808 | 0.823 | 0.865 | 0.886 |
| 7 | Standing Shot Put 8 kg | 0.600 | 0.609 | 0.700 | 0.906 | 0.934 | 0.925 | 0.945 |

In Table 3.2, the results of correlational analysis in strength, jumping, throwing, and running exercises are shown.  In the snatch and clean we see positive relationships only on the first four levels of sports mastery – from the 14m level to the 17m level. Squats were useful for athletes from 14m to 22m. This tendency is also seen in the bench press. In both exercises, a higher level of correlation occurred at the level 17-18m (0.806 and 0.808). In the broad jump, the standing triple jump, the 30m sprint from blocks, and the vertical jump, positive transfer was shown in only the first three levels of sports mastery. The forward shot throw was not included in these but there was transfer for the backward shot throw in the first group.

Table 3.2 – Correlation comparison between indicators of preparedness in male shot putters according to competition result

| No. | Exercise | Sports Result (m), coefficient correlation | | | | | | |
|---|---|---|---|---|---|---|---|---|
| | | 14-15 | 15-16 | 16-17 | 17-18 | 18-19 | 19-20 | 21-22 |
| 1 | Snatch | 0.456 | 0.423 | 0.506 | 0.398 | 0.345 | 0.306 | 0.343 |
| 2 | Clean | 0.506 | 0.487 | 0.450 | 0.432 | 0.342 | 0.305 | 0.291 |
| 3 | Squat | 0.506 | 0.650 | 0.789 | 0.806 | 0.765 | 0.734 | 0.746 |
| 4 | Bench | 0.665 | 0.789 | 0.785 | 0.808 | 0.765 | 0.734 | 0.543 |
| 5 | Standing broad jump | 0.408 | 0.507 | 0.456 | 0.387 | 0.345 | 0.360 | 0.324 |
| 6 | 3 fold jumps | 0.502 | 0.434 | 0.398 | 0.356 | 0.345 | 0.352 | 0.300 |
| 7 | Vertical jump | 0.542 | 0.567 | 0.489 | 0.370 | 0.354 | 0.324 | 0.286 |
| 8 | Forward shot throw | 0.245 | 0.207 | 0.308 | 0.278 | 0.312 | 0.345 | 0.286 |
| 9 | Backward shot throw | 0.405 | 0.398 | 0.308 | 0.276 | 0.342 | 0.309 | 0.290 |

Table 3.3 shows the results of correlational analysis for female shot putters of various levels – from 13 – 20 meters. Here, as in men, there is a positive transfer of training between competition, lighter, and heavier implements. In the shot throw using the 3 and 3.5kg shot there was a

significant correlation for all levels of sports mastery. In most cases, except at one level (17-18m), the correlation was 0.800 or higher. In the shot throw using the 5, 6, and 7.26kg implements, there was a trend for the correlation coefficient to increase as sports mastery increased. Significant increases in the correlation coefficient was observed in the shot throw of the 6kg implement according to sports mastery – 0.567 for the lowest group and 0.900 for the highest group.

Table 3.3 – Correlation comparison between indicators of preparedness in female shot putters along with results for competition, lighter and heavier implements. For levels 1-3, heavier implements were not used as their level of sports mastery did not warrant this means of training.

| Number | Exercise | Sports Result (m), coefficient correlation | | | | | | |
|---|---|---|---|---|---|---|---|---|
| | | 13-14 | 14-15 | 15-16 | 16-17 | 17-18 | 18-19 | 19-20 |
| 1 | Shot Put 3kg | 0.832 | 0.807 | 0.813 | 0.845 | 0.789 | 0.817 | 0.856 |
| 2 | Shot Put 3.5kg | 0.834 | 0.854 | 0.867 | 0.898 | 0.867 | 0.896 | 0.806 |
| 3 | Shot Put 5kg | 0.506 | 0.487 | 0.567 | 0.698 | 0.756 | 0.888 | 0.905 |
| 4 | Shot Put 6kg | - | - | 0.543 | 0.666 | 0.789 | 0.798 | 0.887 |
| 5 | Shot Put 10kg | - | - | - | 0.506 | 0.487 | 0.606 | 0.703 |
| 6 | Standing Shot put 6kg | 0.856 | 0.807 | 0.854 | 0.823 | 0.875 | 0.843 | 0.808 |
| 7 | Standing Shot Put 8 kg | - | - | 0.567 | 0.708 | 0.808 | 0.834 | 0.900 |

In Table 3.4, data for female shot putters in various strength, jumping, running, and throwing exercises is shown. The bench press showed a significant correlation on all levels of sports mastery, the snatch and clean – on the first four levels, and the squat - on the fifth level. Not a single level of sports mastery showed a significant transfer for the forward shot throw and backward shot throw. There were three jumping exercises that showed significant transfer: standing broad jump, three fold broad jumps, and vertical jump. If we compare the correlation coefficient between the competition implements and the lighter or heavier implements with the correlation between the competition implements and all other strength, jumping, and throwing exercises, the lighter or heavier implements have much higher transfer.

Table 3.4 – Correlation comparison between indicators of preparedness in female shot putters according to competition result

| No. | Exercise | Sports Result (m), coefficient correlation | | | | | | |
|-----|----------|-------|-------|-------|-------|-------|-------|-------|
| | | 13-14 | 14-15 | 15-16 | 16-17 | 17-18 | 18-19 | 19-20 |
| 1 | Snatch | 0.578 | 0.465 | 0.532 | 0.524 | 0.367 | 0.376 | 0.359 |
| 2 | Clean | 0.608 | 0.654 | 0.603 | 0.598 | 0.356 | 0.345 | 0.367 |
| 3 | Squat | 0.456 | 0.420 | 0.477 | 0.423 | 0.398 | 0.354 | 0.365 |
| 4 | Bench | 0.563 | 0.588 | 0.543 | 0.660 | 0.705 | 0.687 | 0.589 |
| 5 | Standing broad jump | 0.453 | 0.396 | 0.409 | 0.432 | 0.307 | 0.324 | 0.432 |
| 6 | 3 fold jumps | 0.534 | 0.492 | 0.563 | 0.435 | 0.380 | 0.332 | 0.324 |
| 7 | Vertical jump | 0.566 | 0.435 | 0.406 | 0.376 | 0.354 | 0.332 | 0.342 |
| 8 | Forward shot throw | 0.287 | 0.368 | 0.312 | 0.325 | 0.298 | 0.250 | 0.278 |
| 9 | Backward shot throw | 0.345 | 0.324 | 0.278 | 0.344 | 0.325 | 0.318 | 0.278 |
| 10 | 30 m sprint from blocks | 0.456 | 0.398 | 0.412 | 0.465 | 0.367 | 0.342 | 0.312 |

Table 3.5 shows the correlation coefficient for competition implements and lighter or heavier implements in male discus throwers. These demonstrate that the five implements of varying weight all show a tendency to increase in correlation according to increasing sports mastery of the athlete. Only the 1.5kg disc showed a decrease in correlation as sports mastery increased.

Table 3.5 – Correlation comparison between indicators of preparedness in male discus throwers along with results for competition, lighter and heavier implements

| No. | Exercise | Sport Result (m), Coefficient Correlation | | | | | |
|---|---|---|---|---|---|---|---|
| | | 40-45 | 45-50 | 50-55 | 55-60 | 60-65 | 65-70 |
| 1 | Discus Throw 1.5kg | 0.865 | 0.834 | 0.778 | 0.770 | 0.635 | 0.654 |
| 2 | Discus Throw 1.8kg | 0.802 | 0.856 | 0.876 | 0.932 | 0.908 | 0.912 |
| 3 | Discus Throw 2.25kg | 0.765 | 0.789 | 0.854 | 0.934 | 0.945 | 0.935 |
| 4 | Discus Throw 2.5kg | 0.667 | 0.708 | 0.883 | 0.906 | 0.935 | 0.940 |
| 5 | Standing Shot Throw 3kg | 0.498 | 0.506 | 0.667 | 0.876 | 0.934 | 0.925 |
| 6 | Standing Shot Throw 4kg | 0.435 | 0.444 | 0.589 | 0.847 | 0.921 | 0.934 |

Table 3.6 shows the indicators of correlation between competition results for male discus throwers and their results in several strength, jumping, throwing, and running exercises at six levels of sports mastery – from 40 to 80 meters. This material shows that in all strength exercises there is a positive association in only the first four levels of sports mastery (40-60m). The highest coefficient of correlation was observed in the bench press: the lowest of which was on the first level of sports mastery (0.587) and the best was on the fourth level (0.689). In two of the jumping exercises (broad jump and three fold jumps from a standing start) positive interrelationships are observed on the first three levels of sports mastery (40-55m) and in one exercise (the vertical jump) transfer is observed on the fourth level of sports mastery. There is not a correlation between competition results and results in two of the throwing exercises – the forward and backward shot throws. In two of the first levels of sports mastery, the 30m sprint from blocks also showed transfer.

Table 3.6 – Correlation comparison between indicators of preparedness in male disc throwers according to competition result

| No. | Exer. | Sports Result (m), coefficient correlation | | | | | |
|---|---|---|---|---|---|---|---|
| | | 40-45 | 45-50 | 50-55 | 55-60 | 60-65 | 65-70 |
| 1 | Snatch | 0.406 | 0.456 | 0.506 | 0.409 | 0.345 | 0.323 |
| 2 | Clean | 0.435 | 0.398 | 0.467 | 0.423 | 0.376 | 0.331 |
| 3 | Squat | 0.453 | 0.488 | 0.423 | 0.400 | 0.354 | 0.321 |
| 4 | Bench | 0.587 | 0.645 | 0.634 | 0.689 | 0.381 | 0.306 |
| 5 | Stand broad jump | 0.454 | 0.432 | 0.442 | 0.376 | 0.332 | 0.312 |
| 6 | 3 fold jumps | 0.400 | 0.423 | 0.412 | 0.354 | 0.325 | 0.342 |
| 7 | Vertical jump | 0.432 | 0.453 | 0.408 | 0.454 | 0.376 | 0.356 |
| 8 | Forward shot throw | 0.267 | 0.308 | 0.365 | 0.342 | 0.324 | 0.309 |
| 9 | Backward shot throw | 0.305 | 0.312 | 0.350 | 0.321 | 0.198 | 0.245 |
| 10 | 30m sprint from blocks | 0.398 | 0.405 | 0.345 | 0.320 | 0.365 | 0.325 |

Indicators of correlational relationship in female discus throwers are different and this data is shown in Table 3.7.  The results of throwing a lighter implement (0.75kg) over the course of the first three levels, show a tendency to increase (0.878, 0.867, and 890), but above that level of mastery, the correlation drops down (0.856, 0.805, and 0.750). Using a heavier implement (1.25kg) shows an increasing transfer for more experienced throwers, increasing from one level to the next (0.834, 0.900, and 0.924). A similar dynamic of correlational interrelationship between competition implements and the 1.5 kg implement is observed in the second and greater levels of mastery. There was no transfer observed for the heavier implement with the lowest level of sports mastery (40-45m). On the first two levels of sports mastery, no transfer was observed using the 2kg disc.  In shot throws using the 3kg implement, positive transfer was observed in the second level of mastery (45-50m). This transfer increased as sports mastery increased (0.564, 0.578, 0.790, 0.765, 0.856).

Table 3.7 – Correlation comparison between indicators of preparedness in female disc throwers along with results for competition, lighter and heavier implements

| No. | Exercise | Sports Result (m), coefficient correlation | | | | | |
|-----|----------|-------|-------|-------|-------|-------|-------|
| | | 40-45 | 45-50 | 50-55 | 55-60 | 60-65 | 65-70 |
| 1 | Discus Throw 0.75kg | 0.878 | 0.867 | 0.890 | 0.856 | 0.805 | 0.750 |
| 2 | Discus Throw 1.25kg | 0.567 | 0.675 | 0.768 | 0.834 | 0.900 | 0.924 |
| 3 | Discus Throw 1.5kg | 0.367 | 0.406 | 0.745 | 0.805 | 0.876 | 0.912 |
| 4 | Discus Throw 2kg | 0.345 | 0.378 | 0.606 | 0.756 | 0.806 | 0.865 |
| 5 | Standing Discus Throw 3kg | 0.324 | 0.564 | 0.578 | 0.790 | 0.765 | 0.856 |

In Table 3.8, indicators of correlational relationships in strength, jumping, throwing, and running exercises is shown. On all levels of sports mastery there was positive transfer in three strength exercises – snatch, clean, and bench press. In the squat, there was only a positive transfer for the fourth level of sports mastery – 40 to 60m. In two jumping exercises (broad jump and triple jump from a standing start) positive transfer was observed in the three first levels of sports mastery and in two cases, the vertical jump showed positive transfer. There is no correlation between the two throwing exercises at any level of sports mastery (forward shot throw, backward shot throw).

Table 3.8 – Correlation comparison between indicators of preparedness in female disc throwers according to competition result

| No. | Exercise | Sports Result (m), coefficient correlation | | | | | |
|---|---|---|---|---|---|---|---|
| | | 40-45 | 45-50 | 50-55 | 55-60 | 60-65 | 65-70 |
| 1 | Snatch | 0.678 | 0.624 | 0.653 | 0.589 | 0.545 | 0.504 |
| 2 | Clean | 0.567 | 0.598 | 0.657 | 0.543 | 0.507 | 0.514 |
| 3 | Squat | 0.543 | 0.578 | 0.543 | 0.506 | 0.367 | 0.345 |
| 4 | Bench | 0.408 | 0.546 | 0.664 | 0.654 | 0.607 | 0.580 |
| 5 | Standing broad jump | 0.453 | 0.457 | 0.543 | 0.380 | 0.356 | 0.312 |
| 6 | 3 fold jumps | 0.405 | 0.396 | 0.467 | 0.345 | 0.312 | 0.332 |
| 7 | Vertical jump | 0.456 | 0.423 | 0.380 | 0.345 | 0.342 | 0.309 |
| 8 | Forward shot throw | 0.345 | 0.376 | 0.324 | 0.336 | 0.308 | 0.297 |
| 9 | Backward shot throw | 0.365 | 0.385 | 0.342 | 0.335 | 0.305 | 0.343 |
| 10 | 30m sprint from blocks | 0.423 | 0.456 | 0.324 | 0.365 | 0.312 | 0.345 |

Table 3.9 shows the correlation coefficients between competition weight implements and several lighter or heavier implements for male hammer throwers. These data indicate that on all levels of sports mastery there is positive transfer. If indicators of the hammer throw with the 5kg implement show a positive tendency, then an 8, 9, and 10kg. hammer would produce even more. This is especially true in the higher levels of sports mastery. This applies to the results of the hammer throw with the 8, 9, and 10kg implements. In the hammer throw with the 6kg implement, all levels of sports mastery found that transfer was roughly equal (0.807, 0.786, 0.798, 0.834, 0.804, 0.834, and 0.809).

Table 3.9 – Correlation comparison between indicators of preparedness in male hammer throwers along with results for competition, lighter and heavier implements

| No. | Exercise | Sports Result (m), coefficient correlation | | | | | | |
|---|---|---|---|---|---|---|---|---|
| | | 45-50 | 50-55 | 55-60 | 60-65 | 65-70 | 70-75 | 75-80 |
| 1 | Hammer Throw 5kg | 0.889 | 0.878 | 0.856 | 0.790 | 0.654 | 0.554 | 0.435 |
| 2 | Hammer Throw 6kg | 0.807 | 0.786 | 0.798 | 0.834 | 0.804 | 0.834 | 0809 |
| 3 | Hammer Throw 8kg | 0.397 | 0.435 | 0.567 | 0.704 | 0.897 | 0.905 | 0.954 |
| 4 | Hammer Throw 9kg | - | - | - | 0.665 | 0.789 | 0.896 | 0.932 |
| 5 | Hammer Throw 10 kg | - | - | - | 0.608 | 0.765 | 0.876 | 0.945 |
| 6 | Hammer Throw 16kg | - | - | - | - | 0.406 | 0.398 | 0.489 |

Table. 3.10 shows data that demonstrate strong correlations between the competition implements and several strength, jumping, throwing, and running exercises. These testify to the fact that in the snatch and the jerk there is a positive transfer correlation on all levels of sports mastery. In the squat, this is observed on the first four levels of mastery. A different dynamic of transfer is observed in the three jumping exercises: the broad jump and the three fold jumps showed transfer for the first three levels and the vertical jump, only on the fourth.

Indeed, the correlation here is quite low – 0.440 to 0.550. At the same time, in the two throwing exercises (forward and backward shot throws) positive correlations were not observed on any level of sports mastery. In the 30m sprint from a low start there was transfer on two levels (0.543, 0.509).

Table 3.10 – Correlation comparison between indicators of preparedness in male hammer throwers according to competition result

| No. | Exercise | Sports Result (m), coefficient correlation | | | | | | |
|---|---|---|---|---|---|---|---|---|
| | | 45-50 | 45-55 | 55-60 | 60-65 | 65-70 | 70-75 | 75-80 |
| 1 | Snatch | 0.456 | 0.476 | 0.559 | 0.756 | 0.743 | 0.770 | 0.745 |
| 2 | Clean | 0.555 | 0.607 | 0.578 | 0.700 | 0.698 | 0.543 | 0.707 |
| 3 | Squat | 0.407 | 0.560 | 0.645 | 0.547 | 0.500 | 0.356 | 0.344 |
| 4 | Bench | - | - | - | - | - | - | - |
| 5 | Standing broad jump | 0.409 | 0.456 | 0.445 | 0.380 | 0.365 | 0.370 | 0.345 |
| 6 | 3 fold jumps | 0.435 | 0.487 | 0.434 | 0.376 | 0.324 | 0.344 | 0.305 |
| 7 | Vertical jump | 0.476 | 0.500 | 0.456 | 0.409 | 0.367 | 0.345 | 0.360 |
| 8 | Forward shot throw | 0.287 | 0.300 | 0.256 | 0.276 | 0.265 | 0.356 | 0.317 |
| 9 | Backward shot throw | 0.345 | 0.360 | 0.323 | 0.312 | 0.290 | 0.307 | 0.316 |
| 10 | 30 m sprint from blocks | 0.543 | 0.509 | 0.380 | 0.308 | 0.345 | 0.365 | 0.307 |

Table 3.11 shows experimental material that demonstrates the dynamics of positive transfer between competition results and results in throws of lighter and heavier implements for female hammer throwers. Higher correlation coefficients on all levels of sports mastery were shown in the hammer throw using the two lighter implements (3 and 3.5kg) and in one heavier implement (4.5kg). They fluctuated between 0.800 and 0.900. Given that, in the hammer throw using the 3kg implement, there was a slight decrease of transfer between the two highest levels of sports mastery – 0.800 and 0.786. Higher indicators of correlational relationship were observed in the hammer throw of 4.5kg - 0.856, 0.834, 0.909, 0.913, 0.934, 0.956, and 0.917. In the 5kg and 6kg hammer throw there was a tendency for the correlation coefficient to increase according to the level of sports mastery. Significant correlation coefficients in the competition implement throws are observed in the results of the 7.260kg hammer in the last three levels of sports mastery (0.778, 0.734, and 0.756).

Table 3.11 – Correlation comparison between indicators of preparedness in female hammer throwers along with results for competition, lighter, and heavier implements

| No. | Exercise | Sports Result (m), coefficient correlation | | | | | | |
|-----|----------|-------|-------|-------|-------|-------|-------|-------|
| | | 40-45 | 45-50 | 50-55 | 55-60 | 60-65 | 65-70 | 70-75 |
| 1 | Hammer Throw 3kg | 0.806 | 0.832 | 0.812 | 0.832 | 0.823 | 0.800 | 0.786 |
| 2 | Hammer Throw 3.5kg | 0.846 | 0.876 | 0.835 | 0.906 | 0.886 | 0.908 | 0.898 |
| 3 | Hammer Throw 4.5kg | 0.856 | 0.834 | 0.900 | 0.913 | 0.934 | 0.956 | 0.917 |
| 4 | Hammer Throw 5kg | 0.607 | 0.654 | 0.709 | 0.807 | 0.850 | 0.923 | 0.934 |
| 5 | Hammer Throw 6kg | 0.507 | 0.600 | 0.789 | 0.884 | 0.876 | 0.923 | 0.934 |
| 6 | Hammer Throw 7.26kg | - | - | - | 0.378 | 0.778 | 0.734 | 0.756 |

Table 3.12 – Correlation comparison between indicators of preparedness in female hammer throwers according to competition result

| No. | Exercise | Sports Result (m), coefficient correlation | | | | | | |
|-----|----------|-------|-------|-------|-------|-------|-------|-------|
|     |          | 50-55 | 55-60 | 60-65 | 65-70 | 70-75 | 75-80 | 80-85 |
| 1 | Javelin Throw 0.6kg | 0.845 | 0.856 | 0.823 | 0.802 | 0.765 | 0.784 | 0.700 |
| 2 | Javelin Throw 0.7kg | 0.800 | 0.834 | 0.887 | 0.843 | 0.890 | 0.906 | 0.945 |
| 3 | Javelin Throw 0.9kg | 0.700 | 0.734 | 0.876 | 0.890 | 0.900 | 0.945 | 0.934 |
| 4 | Javelin Throw 1.0kg | - | - | - | 0.835 | 0.887 | 0.906 | 0.923 |
| 5 | Standing Shot Throw 3kg | - | - | - | 0.567 | 0.666 | 0.798 | 0.845 |
| 6 | Standing Shot Throw 4kg | - | - | - | 0.456 | 0.565 | 0.809 | 0.900 |

In Table 3.13, indicators of correlational interrelationships between competition implements and several strength, jumping, throwing, and running exercises are shown. In the snatch, the dynamic of the correlation coefficient from one level of sports mastery to the next was 0.576, 0.607, 0.745, 0.756, 0.734, 0.755 and 0.730. The same type of dynamic was observed in the clean. In the squat, on the first three levels of sports mastery there was in increase in correlation, and then a decrease. There is no correlational relationship on any level of sports mastery between throws of the competition implement and the triple jump from a standing start, the forward and backward shot throws, and the 30m sprint from blocks.

Table 3.13 – Correlation comparison between indicators of preparedness in male javelin throwers along with results for competition, lighter and heavier implements

| No. | Exercise | Sports Result (m), coefficient correlation | | | | | | |
|-----|----------|-------|-------|-------|-------|-------|-------|-------|
|     |          | 40-45 | 45-50 | 50-55 | 55-60 | 60-65 | 65-70 | 70-75 |
| 1 | Snatch | 0.576 | 0.607 | 0.745 | 0.756 | 0.734 | 0.755 | 0.730 |
| 2 | Clean | 0.487 | 0.567 | 0.666 | 0.643 | 0.709 | 0.678 | 0.700 |
| 3 | Squat | 0.598 | 0.634 | 0.665 | 0.634 | 0.608 | 0.578 | 0.432 |
| 4 | Standing broad jump | 0.435 | 0.450 | 0.370 | 0.345 | 0.356 | 0.324 | 0.312 |
| 5 | 3 fold jumps | 0.367 | 0.325 | 0.324 | 0.300 | 0.287 | 0.265 | 0.307 |
| 6 | Vertical jump | 0.398 | 0.456 | 0.500 | 0.421 | 0.367 | 0.324 | 0.305 |
| 7 | Forward shot throw | 0.356 | 0.324 | 0.360 | 0.289 | 0.340 | 0.298 | 0.265 |
| 8 | Backward shot throw | 0.312 | 0.345 | 0.360 | 0.312 | 0.345 | 0.322 | 0.344 |
| 9 | 30 m sprint from blocks | 0.378 | 0.369 | 0.345 | 0.350 | 0.342 | 0.323 | 0.345 |

In Table 3.14 correlational analysis of male javelin throwers of varying sport qualification in several strength, jumping, throwing, and running exercises is shown. It is of special significance that only the results in the snatch correlate with the results in the throws with the competition implement on all five levels of sports mastery. On four levels of there was a positive correlation in the clean, as well as for three jumping exercises (broad jump, triple jump from a standing start, vertical jump) and the 30m sprint from blocks. In the two throwing exercises (forward and backward shot throws) correlational relationships were not observed.

Table 3.14 – Correlational comparison between indicators of preparedness in male javelin throwers according to competition result

| No. | Exercise | Sports Result (m), coefficient correlation | | | | | | |
|---|---|---|---|---|---|---|---|---|
| | | 50-55 | 55-60 | 60-65 | 65-70 | 70-75 | 75-80 | 80-85 |
| 1 | Snatch | 0.498 | 0.436 | 0.507 | 0.437 | 0.395 | 0.345 | 0.320 |
| 2 | Clean | 0.435 | 0.497 | 0.466 | 0.408 | 0.345 | 0.323 | 0346 |
| 3 | Squat | 0.456 | 0.476 | 0.504 | 0.342 | 0.323 | 0.312 | 0.287 |
| 4 | Bench | 0.396 | 0.306 | 0.345 | 0.342 | 0.312 | 0.296 | 0.345 |
| 5 | Standing broad jump | 0.405 | 0.467 | 0.534 | 0.407 | 0.380 | 0.354 | 0.321 |
| 6 | 3 fold jumps | 0.445 | 0.456 | 0.412 | 0.456 | 0.367 | 0.345 | 0.342 |
| 7 | Vertical jump | 0.423 | 0.400 | 0.432 | 0.396 | 0.321 | 0.330 | 0.342 |
| 8 | Forward shot throw | 0.342 | 0.334 | 0.365 | 0.312 | 0.342 | 0.305 | 0.290 |
| 9 | Backward shot throw | 0.367 | 0.324 | 0.345 | 0.308 | 0.332 | 0.313 | 0.290 |
| 10 | 30 m sprint from blocks | 0.456 | 0.405 | 0.435 | 0.486 | 0.380 | 0.345 | 0.304 |

Table 3.15 shows indicators of correlational analysis between competition, lighter, and heavier implements in the javelin for various levels of sports mastery. For the 0.5kg implement, on all levels of sports mastery there was positive transfer, with a correlation coefficient that remained

roughly the same for all groups (around 0.900). For the heavier implements (0.7 and 0.8kg, and 2.0 and 3.0kg standing throw) we see a significant upward trend in correlation as sports mastery increases. For example, in the 0.8kg implement - 0.398, 0.476, 0.565, 0.678, 0.800, and 0.856,

Table 3.15 – Correlational comparison between indicators of preparedness in female javelin throwers along with results for competition, lighter and heavier implements

| No. | Exercise | Sports Result (m), coefficient correlation | | | | | |
|-----|----------|-------|-------|-------|-------|-------|-------|
|     |          | 40-45 | 45-50 | 50-55 | 55-60 | 60-65 | 65-70 |
| 1 | Javelin Throw 0.5kg | 0.876 | 0.834 | 0.856 | 0.905 | 0.876 | 0.904 |
| 2 | Javelin Throw 0.7kg | 0.564 | 0.676 | 0.785 | 0.798 | 0.905 | 0.923 |
| 3 | Javelin Throw 0.8kg | 0.398 | 0.476 | 0.565 | 0.678 | 0.800 | 0.856 |
| 4 | Standing Shot Throw 2kg | 0.390 | 0.412 | 0.598 | 0.745 | 0.798 | 0.823 |
| 5 | Standing Shot Throw 3kg | 0.354 | 0.423 | 0.456 | 0.723 | 0.790 | 0.805 |

Table 3.16 shows the correlation coefficients between competition implements and several strength, jumping, throwing, and running exercises. We will begin with the three strength exercises. Positive transfer was observed on all levels of sports mastery in only the snatch. In the clean and in the squat, positive transfer was only observed in the three first

levels of sports mastery. Even there, the correlation coefficient was weak – between 0.423 and 0.598. In jumps from a standing start, positive transfer was only observed in the four first levels of sports mastery. Here, the highest coefficients were 0.500, 0.543, 0.512, and 0.465. In the forward and backward shot throws there was no transfer observed for any athlete, regardless of sports mastery.

Table 3.16 – Correlation comparison between indicators of preparedness in female javelin throwers according to competition result

| No. | Exercise | Sports Result (m), coefficient correlation | | | | | |
|---|---|---|---|---|---|---|---|
| | | 40-45 | 45-50 | 50-55 | 55-60 | 60-65 | 65-70 |
| 1 | Snatch | 0.564 | 0.603 | 0.587 | 0.598 | 0.500 | 0.523 |
| 2 | Clean | 0.476 | 0.507 | 0.423 | 0.376 | 0.345 | 0.354 |
| 3 | Squat | 0.457 | 0.435 | 0.534 | 0.366 | 0.343 | 0.312 |
| 4 | Standing broad jump | 0.400 | 0.453 | 0.412 | 0.397 | 0.365 | 0.372 |
| 5 | 3 fold jumps | 0.454 | 0.475 | 0.434 | 0.453 | 0.350 | 0.365 |
| 6 | Vertical jump | 0.500 | 0.543 | 0.512 | 0.465 | 0.354 | 0.300 |
| 7 | Forward shot throw | 0.345 | 0.321 | 0.369 | 0.324 | 0.298 | 0.315 |
| 8 | Backward shot throw | 0.322 | 0.300 | 0.278 | 0.354 | 0.309 | 0.365 |
| 9 | 30m sprint from blocks | 0.500 | 0.465 | 0.523 | 0.489 | 0.400 | 0.365 |

In the theory and practice of track and field throws, more often than not, the following test exercises are used for monitoring the progress of throwers: snatch, clean, squat, bench press, standing broad jump, standing three fold broad jump, vertical jump, forward and backward shot throw, and 30m sprints from blocks. Amongst these test exercises and results in competition exercises, specialists seek to find positive correlational relationships indicative of long term adaptations being acquired by the systems of the athlete, at all levels of sports mastery. Respectively, comparing the characteristics of the best and worst results in these given test indicators can help achieve a significant level of development where sports results will grow from one level of sports mastery to the next.

Table 3.17 shows the indicators for the best and worst results in test indicators for shot putters of various sports qualification. In strength exercises, the highest variation was found for the following: the snatch – 25kg, the clean – 50kg, and the bench press – 52.5kg. In the standing broad jump, the highest difference between the best and worst results was at the 15-16m level (42cm) and the lowest (13cm), was seen at the 18-19m level. In the three fold broad jump from a standing start, the difference was 47cm at the 21-22m level and 30cm at the 15-18m levels. Lower differences were observed in the vertical jump. Their dynamics from one level of sports mastery to the next were respectively as follows: 13, 18, 15, 15, 14, 10, and 12cm. The best and worst indicators for the forward shot throw were significant in one case – 3m in the 18-19m group and only 160cm in the 14-15m group.

The smallest difference was observed in the backwards shot throw. On the 18-19m level, it differed 256cm; on the 15-16m level – 111cm. Only on the two first levels of sports mastery did the difference between the best and worst indicators show transfer in the 30m sprint from blocks.

Table 3.17 – Comparison of characteristics for the best (1) and worst (2) results in male hammer throwers in several strength, jumping, and throwing exercises.

| No. | Exercise | BW | Sports Result (m) | | | | | | |
|---|---|---|---|---|---|---|---|---|---|
| | | | 14-15 | 15-16 | 16-17 | 17-18 | 18-19 | 19-20 | 21-22 |
| 1 | Snatch | 1 | 100 | 110 | 120 | 135 | 140 | 155 | 155 |
| | | 2 | 75 | 75 | 95 | 100 | 110 | 115 | 120 |
| 2 | Clean | 1 | 140 | 145 | 155 | 160 | 165 | 185 | 185 |
| | | 2 | 120 | 120 | 125 | 125 | 130 | 135 | 140 |
| 3 | Squat | 1 | 170 | 190 | 225 | 240 | 275 | 280 | 300 |
| | | 2 | 140 | 145 | 185 | 190 | 195 | 205 | 220 |
| 4 | Bench Press | 1 | 130 | 140 | 165 | 190 | 210 | 245 | 305 |
| | | 2 | 100 | 105 | 115 | 135 | 150 | 185 | 220 |
| 5 | Standing Broad Jump (cm) | 1 | 323 | 321 | 331 | 320 | 325 | 340 | 336 |
| | | 2 | 295 | 290 | 289 | 302 | 312 | 309 | 305 |
| 6 | Triple Jump standing Start (cm) | 1 | 923 | 932 | 912 | 934 | 923 | 925 | 936 |
| | | 2 | 888 | 902 | 876 | 904 | 889 | 890 | 889 |
| 7 | Vertical Jump (cm) | 1 | 78 | 79 | 75 | 77 | 78 | 76 | 78 |
| | | 2 | 65 | 61 | 60 | 62 | 64 | 66 | 62 |
| 8 | Forward shot Throw (m) | 1 | 16.7 | 17.0 | 17.8 | 18.5 | 20.4 | 20.1 | 19.8 |
| | | 2 | 15.1 | 15.5 | 15.7 | 16 | 17.2 | 17.7 | 17.4 |
| 9 | Backward shot Throw (m) | 1 | 20.1 | 19.87 | 20.0 | 20.5 | 22.1 | 22.3 | 21.3 |
| | | 2 | 18.66 | 18.76 | 17.8 | 18.0 | 19.5 | 20.0 | 19.8 |
| 10 | 30m sprint from blocks | 1 | 3.8 | 3.9 | 3.9 | 3.8 | 4.2 | 4.1 | 4.2 |
| | | 2 | 4.3 | 4.4 | 4.2 | 4.1 | 4.4 | 4.3 | 4.5 |

Table 3.18 shows a comparison between the best and worst indicators in strength, jumping, throwing, and running exercises in the female shot putters at several levels of sports mastery. The largest difference between the best and worst indicators was in the strength exercises. When we look at the results from a perspective of percent change, there is a large difference in the snatch compared to the other strength exercises. In the standing broad jump, the largest difference between the best and worst results was observed on the 15-16m level where it was 42cm and the smallest difference was 12cm, at the 17-18cm level. A more significant difference was observed in the percent change in the vertical jumps. On the first and third levels of sports mastery it differed 23cm and only 8cm on the second level. In the forward and backward shot throws, the best and worst results fluctuated from one level of sports mastery to another. This tendency was not observed in the worst results. In the backward shot throw, the change in results from one level of mastery to the next began in the 14-15m group. If we compare the best and worst indicators in the 30m sprint from blocks according to increasing mastery, athletes tended to get faster by about 0.1 – 0.2 seconds per level of mastery.

Table 3.18 – Comparison of characteristics for the best (1) and worst (2) results in female shot putters in several strength, jumping, and throwing exercises.

| No. | Exercise | BW | Sports Result (m) | | | | | | |
|-----|----------|----|----|----|----|----|----|----|----|
| | | | 13-14 | 14-15 | 15-16 | 16-17 | 17-18 | 18-19 | 19-20 |
| 1 | Snatch | 1 | 70 | 70 | 75 | 75 | 80 | 85 | 90 |
| | | 2 | 50 | 50 | 50 | 55 | 60 | 60 | 75 |
| 2 | Clean | 1 | 85 | 85 | 90 | 85 | 90 | 100 | 105 |
| | | 2 | 65 | 70 | 75 | 75 | 80 | 85 | 90 |
| 3 | Squat | 1 | 130 | 140 | 150 | 165 | 175 | 180 | 190 |
| | | 2 | 120 | 120 | 120 | 130 | 140 | 150 | 150 |
| 4 | Bench Press | 1 | 90 | 95 | 110 | 110 | 125 | 140 | 150 |
| | | 2 | 75 | 80 | 80 | 85 | 90 | 110 | 120 |
| 5 | Standing Broad Jump (cm) | 1 | 276 | 270 | 287 | 276 | 265 | 270 | 277 |
| | | 2 | 245 | 250 | 245 | 247 | 253 | 245 | 253 |
| 6 | Triple Jump standing Start (cm) | 1 | 798 | 785 | 795 | 806 | 810 | 820 | 798 |
| | | 2 | 756 | 765 | 754 | 765 | 745 | 765 | 744 |
| 7 | Vertical Jump (cm) | 1 | 78 | 75 | 77 | 83 | 81 | 80 | 81 |
| | | 2 | 55 | 67 | 65 | 60 | 63 | 60 | 66 |
| 8 | Forward shot Throw (m) | 1 | 15.6 | 16.7 | 17.5 | 18.0 | 19.0 | 19.3 | 19.4 |
| | | 2 | 15.0 | 15.7 | 16.6 | 16.0 | 17.4 | 17.0 | 16.8 |
| 9 | Backward shot Throw (m) | 1 | 18.5 | 18.3 | 18.9 | 19.6 | 20.0 | 20.4 | 21.1 |
| | | 2 | 17.3 | 17.0 | 18.0 | 18.3 | 19.0 | 19.0 | 19.0 |
| 10 | 30m sprint from blocks | 1 | 4.3 | 4.3 | 4.2 | 4.2 | 43 | 4.3 | 4.2 |
| | | 2 | 4.6 | 4.5 | 4.4 | 4.5 | 4.6 | 4.5 | 4.4 |

Table 3.19 shows the dynamics of the best and worst results in several strength, jumping, throwing, and running exercises for male discus throwers at various levels of sports mastery. In strength exercises, the largest difference between the best and worst indicators was observed in the snatch (in terms of percent change) compared to indicators in the clean, the squat, and the bench press. This is in reference to the trend of the indicators from one level of sports mastery to another. If a detailed analysis is taken, the largest difference in the snatch is in the first three levels (40-45, 45-50, and 50-55m), in the clean - on the following level (60-65m), and in the squat and bench press the difference was 40kg and 50kg, respectively. If we compare the difference between the best and worst indicators of the three jumping exercises (broad jump, standing start triple jump, and vertical jump), then we see that the percent change is insignificant in comparison to the change in the strength exercises. In the forward shot throw there is a significant tendency for growth of the best and worst indicators from one level of sports mastery to the next. One exception in the 50-55m level of sports mastery is seen, where the lower level of sports mastery has a slightly higher result. Dynamics of the best indicators in the backward shot throw had a waving character (18.97, 18.65, 19.06, 18.65, 20.67 and 21.56m), and the worst – in five cases, the indicators increased with sports mastery and in one case, decreased. For the 30m sprint from blocks, the results are fairly similar for all levels of sports mastery.

Table 3.19 – Comparison of characteristics for the best (1) and worst (2) results in male discus throwers in several strength, jumping, and throwing exercises.

| N. | Exercise | Sports Result (m) | | | | | | |
|---|---|---|---|---|---|---|---|---|
| | | Class | 40-45 | 45-50 | 50-55 | 55-60 | 60-65 | 65-70 |
| 1 | Snatch | 1 | 90 | 100 | 120 | 130 | 135 | 140 |
| | | 2 | 75 | 80 | 95 | 105 | 110 | 120 |
| 2 | Clean | 1 | 130 | 130 | 140 | 170 | 170 | 175 |
| | | 2 | 110 | 110 | 115 | 145 | 140 | 145 |
| 3 | Squat | 1 | 160 | 160 | 170 | 180 | 220 | 250 |
| | | 2 | 140 | 145 | 145 | 150 | 190 | 210 |
| 4 | Bench Press | 1 | 120 | 130 | 140 | 170 | 200 | 250 |
| | | 2 | 100 | 110 | 110 | 130 | 160 | 200 |
| 5 | Standing Broad Jump (cm) | 1 | 318 | 342 | 335 | 345 | 356 | 344 |
| | | 2 | 295 | 309 | 302 | 312 | 320 | 323 |
| 6 | Triple Jump standing Start (cm) | 1 | 926 | 943 | 921 | 934 | 940 | 344 |
| | | 2 | 890 | 896 | 876 | 900 | 912 | 323 |
| 7 | Vertical Jump (cm) | 1 | 86 | 80 | 85 | 90 | 84 | 86 |
| | | 2 | 70 | 71 | 72 | 75 | 73 | 72 |
| 8 | Forward shot Throw (m) | 1 | 16.0 | 16.3 | 16.7 | 17.0 | 19.0 | 19.8 |
| | | 2 | 15.4 | 16.0 | 15.8 | 16.1 | 17.3 | 17.9 |
| 9 | Backward shot Throw (m) | 1 | 18.9 | 18.6 | 19.0 | 18.6 | 20.6 | 21.5 |
| | | 2 | 18.0 | 18.2 | 18.3 | 18.0 | 19.4 | 19.9 |
| 10 | 30m sprint from blocks | 1 | 3.8 | 3.8 | 4.0 | 4.1 | 4.1 | 4.0 |
| | | 2 | 4.2 | 4.1 | 4.3 | 4.3 | 4.3 | 4.2 |

Table 3.20 shows the best and worst indicators for several strength, jumping, throwing, and running exercises on various levels of sports mastery in female discus throwers. In the snatch, the largest difference between the best and worst result was similar to that of the bench press. Also, the front squat and the cleans were similar in terms of the difference between indicators. In all cases, the results we just discussed are based on the percentage change. In three jumping exercises the largest difference between best and worst indicators was in the standing broad jump. In the forward and backward shot throws, the dynamics of the best and worst indicators trended upward according to the level of sports mastery of the athlete. For the worst results, only in one case (at the 45-50m level) were results observed to decline in the forward and backward shot throws. On the fifth level of sports mastery, the difference between the best and worst indicators fluctuated between 0.1 and 0.2 seconds, and in the first case this difference rose above 0.3 seconds.

Table 3.20 – Comparison of characteristics for the best (1) and worst (2) results in female discus throwers in several strength, jumping, and throwing exercises.

| No. | Exercise | | Sports Result (m) | | | | | |
|---|---|---|---|---|---|---|---|---|
| | | Class | 40-45 | 45-50 | 50-55 | 55-60 | 60-65 | 65-70 |
| 1 | Snatch | 1 | 70 | 72.5 | 75 | 80 | 85 | 100 |
| | | 2 | 55 | 55 | 60 | 60 | 70 | 80 |
| 2 | Clean | 1 | 80 | 80 | 85 | 90 | 100 | 110 |
| | | 2 | 60 | 70 | 70 | 75 | 80 | 90 |
| 3 | Squat | 1 | 125 | 135 | 135 | 140 | 160 | 175 |
| | | 2 | 100 | 100 | 110 | 115 | 130 | 150 |
| 4 | Bench Press | 1 | 80 | 80 | 90 | 120 | 130 | 145 |
| | | 2 | 70 | 75 | 75 | 100 | 110 | 125 |
| 5 | Standing Broad Jump (cm) | 1 | 280 | 275 | 271 | 278 | 277 | 270 |
| | | 2 | 240 | 234 | 230 | 232 | 240 | 243 |
| 6 | Triple Jump standing Start (cm) | 1 | 787 | 790 | 795 | 801 | 823 | 815 |
| | | 2 | 734 | 756 | 766 | 757 | 769 | 743 |
| 7 | Vertical Jump (cm) | 1 | 82 | 80 | 77 | 79 | 80 | 79 |
| | | 2 | 60 | 65 | 63 | 59 | 62 | 70 |
| 8 | Forward shot Throw (m) | 1 | 16.7 | 16.8 | 17.1 | 18.8 | 18.9 | 19.6 |
| | | 2 | 16.3 | 15.1 | 16.3 | 17.3 | 17.7 | 18.0 |
| 9 | Backward shot Throw (m) | 1 | 18.7 | 18.7 | 19.0 | 20.2 | 20.9 | 20.5 |
| | | 2 | 17.9 | 17.7 | 18.0 | 18.8 | 19.6 | 19.5 |
| 10 | 30m sprint from blocks | 1 | 4.1 | 4.0 | 4.2 | 4.2 | 4.1 | 4.1 |
| | | 2 | 4.4 | 4.2 | 4.4 | 4.1 | 4.3 | 4.2 |

Table 3.21 shows experimental data that displays a strong relationship between the difference in the best and worst indicators for various strength, jumping, throwing, and running exercises in male hammer throwers of various sport qualification. Above all, it demonstrates that in three strength exercises, the best results increase as sports mastery increases. A similar trend among the worst results from one level of mastery to the next is only observed in the snatch. In the cleans and the front squat, on the first level of sports mastery, these strength numbers leveled off and subsequently increased. The greatest difference between the best and worst indicators by percent change was in the snatch. In the standing broad jump, on the second level of sports mastery (50-55m), there was a large difference between best and worst indicators at 40cm. By percentage change, there was a small difference for the standing triple jump. The difference between the best and worst indicators for the results in the vertical jump were varied: 10, 9 ,15, 12, 7, 14, and 9cm, respectively. In the forward and backward shot throws, the best results increased from one level of sports mastery to the next. The dynamic of the worst results in several cases had a tendency to decrease when compared to the first two levels. The largest difference was observed at the level of 65-70m – 1.91m. The following dynamic in the difference between best and worst indicators in the 30m sprint was observed: 0.3, 0.4, 0.2, 0.3, 0.1, 0.2 and 0.1 sec.

Table 3.21 – Comparison of characteristics for the best (1) and worst (2) results in male hammer throwers in several strength, jumping, and throwing exercises.

| No. | Exercise | BW | Sports Result (m) | | | | | | |
|---|---|---|---|---|---|---|---|---|---|
| | | | 45-50 | 50-55 | 55-60 | 60-65 | 65-70 | 70-75 | 75-80 |
| 1 | Snatch | 1 | 75 | 75 | 85 | 90 | 110 | 120 | 145 |
| | | 2 | 60 | 65 | 70 | 80 | 95 | 100 | 110 |
| 2 | Clean | 1 | 120 | 120 | 125 | 130 | 140 | 150 | 165 |
| | | 2 | 105 | 110 | 110 | 110 | 115 | 115 | 115 |
| 3 | Squat | 1 | 130 | 140 | 160 | 190 | 200 | 230 | 230 |
| | | 2 | 120 | 120 | 130 | 150 | 160 | 170 | 190 |
| 4 | Bench Press | 1 | - | - | - | - | - | - | - |
| | | 2 | | | | | | | |
| 5 | Standing Broad Jump (cm) | 1 | 323 | 345 | 325 | 332 | 312 | 315 | 330 |
| | | 2 | 298 | 305 | 307 | 300 | 301 | 299 | 309 |
| 6 | Triple Jump standing Start (cm) | 1 | 890 | 876 | 905 | 912 | 930 | 925 | 932 |
| | | 2 | 876 | 845 | 887 | 890 | 894 | 900 | 902 |
| 7 | Vertical Jump (cm) | 1 | 86 | 82 | 90 | 85 | 82 | 84 | 81 |
| | | 2 | 76 | 73 | 75 | 73 | 75 | 70 | 72 |
| 8 | Forward shot Throw (m) | 1 | 16.5 | 16.4 | 16.8 | 16.9 | 17.9 | 18.5 | 19.2 |
| | | 2 | 15.8 | 15.4 | 15.8 | 15.9 | 16.0 | 17.5 | 18.3 |
| 9 | Backward shot Throw (m) | 1 | 18.9 | 17.9 | 18.5 | 18.7 | 19.5 | 19.9 | 21.1 |
| | | 2 | 17.6 | 17.4 | 17.8 | 17.3 | 18.0 | 18.4 | 19.9 |
| 10 | 30m sprint from blocks | 1 | 3.9 | 3.8 | 4.0 | 3.9 | 4.0 | 4.0 | 4.0 |
| | | 2 | 4.2 | 4.2 | 4.2 | 4.2 | 4.1 | 4.2 | 4.1 |

Table 3.22 shows the dynamic of the best and worst results in various types of exercises for hammer throwers of various levels of sports mastery. In the third and fourth exercises there is a similar dynamic of best sports results from one level of mastery to the next. It has a tendency to increase, albeit, in a few cases the increase is quite small. In contrast, the results in the snatch show a continual increase as mastery increases. Differences between best results are as follows: 80, 80, 100, 120, 110, 120, 120 kg. The largest difference between best and worst indicators in the percent change was seen in the snatch as well (between 10-20% for all groups). In the standing broad jump, the largest change was observed at 37cm in the 60-65m group. In the triple jump from a standing start, the difference was quite a bit larger: over 50cm in most cases, but not as significant according to percent change. In the vertical jump, there was a difference observed on all levels of sports mastery as follows: 10, 11, 10, 13, 12, 8, and 12 cm. In the forward shot throw, the largest difference between best and worst indicators were 136cm and in the backward shot throw – 116cm. The dynamics of change for the best results in the 30m sprint from blocks on all levels of sports mastery were altogether insignificant. The dynamics of the worst results also did not differ much from one another. In three cases, the difference between the best and worst indicators reached 0.3 seconds, and in one case, 0.1 seconds.

Table 3.22 – Comparison of characteristics for the best (1) and worst (2) results in female hammer throwers in several strength, jumping, and throwing exercises.

| No. | Exercise | B W | Sports Result (m) | | | | | | |
|---|---|---|---|---|---|---|---|---|---|
| | | | 45-50 | 50-55 | 55-60 | 60-65 | 65-70 | 70-75 | 75-80 |
| 1 | Snatch | 1 | 55 | 55 | 60 | 60 | 65 | 75 | 80 |
| | | 2 | 45 | 40 | 50 | 45 | 50 | 60 | 60 |
| 2 | Clean | 1 | 65 | 65 | 70 | 80 | 80 | 90 | 90 |
| | | 2 | 55 | 55 | 55 | 60 | 55 | 70 | 70 |
| 3 | Squat | 1 | 90 | 90 | 100 | 120 | 120 | 130 | 140 |
| | | 2 | 80 | 85 | 85 | 100 | 110 | 110 | 120 |
| 4 | Bench Press | 1 | 60 | 70 | 75 | 80 | 80 | 85 | 90 |
| | | 2 | 50 | 55 | 65 | 70 | 70 | 70 | 80 |
| 5 | Standing Broad Jump (cm) | 1 | 265 | 260 | 257 | 278 | 280 | 265 | 270 |
| | | 2 | 234 | 235 | 221 | 265 | 243 | 242 | 256 |
| 6 | Triple Jump standing Start (cm) | 1 | 789 | 800 | 795 | 786 | 810 | 806 | 813 |
| | | 2 | 756 | 747 | 753 | 747 | 760 | 761 | 777 |
| 7 | Vertical Jump (cm) | 1 | 75 | 77 | 74 | 72 | 75 | 74 | 72 |
| | | 2 | 66 | 62 | 60 | 62 | 60 | 64 | 62 |
| 8 | Forward shot Throw (m) | 1 | 15.8 | 16.8 | 17.4 | 17.0 | 17.5 | 17.4 | 18.4 |
| | | 2 | 15.2 | 15.7 | 15.9 | 16.2 | 16.7 | 16.2 | 16.6 |
| 9 | Backward shot Throw (m) | 1 | 18.2 | 17.4 | 18.8 | 18.6 | 19.0 | 19.3 | 20.0 |
| | | 2 | 17.7 | 16.8 | 17.4 | 17.0 | 18.2 | 18.8 | 18.7 |
| 10 | 30m sprint from blocks | 1 | 4.2 | 4.1 | 4.2 | 4.1 | 4.1 | 4.2 | 4.1 |
| | | 2 | 4.5 | 4.5 | 4.4 | 4.4 | 4.2 | 4.3 | 4.3 |

Table 3.23 shows experimental material that highlights a significant relationship between the best and worst indicators for several strength jumping, throwing, and running exercises on various levels of sports mastery in male javelin throwers. In the snatch, the largest difference was in the third and fifth levels of sports mastery. This dynamic shifted in the clean; there was very little difference between different levels of sports mastery. Again, no significant difference was seen according to sports mastery in the back squat. In the bench press the difference between best and worst indicators went from as low as 10kg to as much as 25kg. Of the three jumps, the largest difference according to percent change was observed in the vertical jump. In the standing broad jump the difference reached 42cm in the highest qualified athletes and in the standing start triple jump – 43cm. In the shot throw forward and backward there was a tendency for the best results to increase according to sports mastery. A different dynamic was seen in the worst results: in five cases it increased, and in one case (fourth level) it decreased compared to the previous group. In the backward shot throw, the relationship was non-linear, with some groups experiencing a 0.2 second change and others only a 0.1 second change.

Table 3.23 – Comparison of characteristics for the best (1) and worst (2) results in male javelin throwers in several strength, jumping, and throwing exercises.

| No. | Exercise | BW | Sports Result (m) | | | | | | |
|---|---|---|---|---|---|---|---|---|---|
| | | | 50-55 | 55-60 | 60-65 | 65-70 | 70-75 | 75-80 | 80-85 |
| 1 | Snatch | 1 | 75 | 80 | 80 | 85 | 90 | 95 | 110 |
| | | 2 | 60 | 70 | 70 | 70 | 80 | 80 | 90 |
| 2 | Clean | 1 | 100 | 110 | 115 | 115 | 125 | 125 | 140 |
| | | 2 | 85 | 85 | 90 | 95 | 95 | 95 | 115 |
| 3 | Squat | 1 | 120 | 120 | 135 | 145 | 160 | 175 | 175 |
| | | 2 | 110 | 100 | 110 | 125 | 130 | 130 | 149 |
| 4 | Bench Press | 1 | 80 | 80 | 100 | 120 | 110 | 120 | 120 |
| | | 2 | 70 | 70 | 90 | 100 | 100 | 110 | 110 |
| 5 | Standing Broad Jump (cm) | 1 | 321 | 345 | 326 | 332 | 324 | 342 | 329 |
| | | 2 | 300 | 312 | 289 | 298 | 305 | 312 | 309 |
| 6 | Triple Jump standing Start (cm) | 1 | 906 | 923 | 917 | 934 | 943 | 923 | 932 |
| | | 2 | 888 | 897 | 879 | 887 | 901 | 903 | 900 |
| 7 | Vertical Jump (cm) | 1 | 85 | 87 | 90 | 89 | 87 | 86 | 88 |
| | | 2 | 75 | 76 | 80 | 76 | 75 | 78 | 76 |
| 8 | Forward shot Throw (m) | 1 | 16.3 | 16.5 | 16.4 | 17.1 | 17.4 | 17.0 | 17.5 |
| | | 2 | 15.5 | 15.7 | 15.9 | 16.5 | 16.0 | 16.6 | 16.8 |
| 9 | Backward shot Throw (m) | 1 | 18.6 | 19.0 | 18.5 | 19.3 | 19.0 | 19.3 | 19.2 |
| | | 2 | 17.7 | 18.2 | 17.7 | 18.5 | 18.4 | 18.6 | 18.0 |
| 10 | 30m sprint from blocks | 1 | 3.8 | 3.8 | 3.9 | 3.9 | 3.8 | 3.8 | 3.8 |
| | | 2 | 4.1 | 4.0 | 4.2 | 4.0 | 4.0 | 4.1 | 4.0 |

In Table 3.24, data that demonstrates the essential difference between best and worst results in several strength, power, jumping and running exercises for female throwers of the javelin is shown. In two cases, for both the 50-55m group and the 55-60m group, the difference is greater than 15kg; in two more cases, it's greater than 10kg, and one case the difference was only 5kg. In the clean, the difference between the best and worst groups were as follows: 5kg (40-45m group), 10kg (45-50m group), 15kg (50-55m group), 10kg (55-60m group), 10kg (60-65m group), and 10kg (65-70m group). In the squat, only in the last group of sports mastery (65-70m) was there a difference of 20kg. In four other cases (groups 40-55m, 45-50m, 55-60m, and 60-65m) the difference was over 10kg and only in one case was it 5 kg (50-55m.). The greatest difference among the four strength indicators was observed both in percent and in kilos lifted for the bench press: 15, 10, 15, 15, 25, and 20 kg, respectively. Similar differences were observed in the three jumping exercises. Again, the largest difference by percent and by metric indicators was in the vertical jump: 17, 20, 20, 9, 10 and 14 cm. In the forward shot throw, the dynamics between the best and worst results from one level of sports mastery to another had a tendency to increase; also, the difference between them was small. For example, only in the lowest level of sports mastery was 80cm reached. In the backwards shot throw, the dynamics of the best and worst results had a more sporadic distribution. The largest difference was observed for the 60-65m group at 100cm. The difference between the best and worst results for the 30m sprint from blocks was only observed in two cases (in the 40-45m group and the 50-55 m group) at 0.2 seconds and 0.1 seconds.

Table 3.24 – Comparison of characteristics for the best (1) and worst (2) results in female javelin throwers in several strength, jumping, and throwing exercises.

| No. | Exercise | BW | Sports Result (m) | | | | | |
|-----|----------|----|-------|-------|------|-------|-------|-------|
| | | | 40-45 | 45-50 | 50-5 | 55-60 | 60-65 | 65-70 |
| 1 | Snatch | 1 | 55 | 50 | 55 | 65 | 65 | 75 |
| | | 2 | 45 | 45 | 40 | 55 | 50 | 65 |
| 2 | Clean | 1 | 70 | 70 | 75 | 80 | 80 | 85 |
| | | 2 | 65 | 60 | 60 | 70 | 70 | 75 |
| 3 | Squat | 1 | 80 | 80 | 80 | 90 | 110 | 120 |
| | | 2 | 70 | 70 | 75 | 80 | 100 | 100 |
| 4 | Bench Press | 1 | 60 | 60 | 75 | 80 | 85 | 90 |
| | | 2 | 45 | 50 | 60 | 65 | 60 | 70 |
| 5 | Standing Broad Jump (cm) | 1 | 253 | 245 | 256 | 252 | 270 | 267 |
| | | 2 | 235 | 221 | 232 | 231 | 243 | 225 |
| 6 | Triple Jump standing Start (cm) | 1 | 756 | 765 | 788 | 800 | 797 | 799 |
| | | 2 | 730 | 734 | 761 | 766 | 754 | 765 |
| 7 | Vertical Jump (cm) | 1 | 85 | 85 | 90 | 83 | 86 | 87 |
| | | 2 | 68 | 65 | 70 | 74 | 76 | 73 |
| 8 | Forward shot Throw (m) | 1 | 15.4 | 15.7 | 16.0 | 16.1 | 16.3 | 16.7 |
| | | 2 | 15.0 | 15.3 | 15.6 | 15.7 | 15.7 | 15.9 |
| 9 | Backward shot Throw (m) | 1 | 17.5 | 17.8 | 17.3 | 17.9 | 18.5 | 18.0 |
| | | 2 | 16.2 | 16.7 | 16.7 | 17.0 | 17.5 | 17.3 |
| 10 | 30m sprint from blocks | 1 | 4.2 | 4.2 | 4.1 | 4.2 | 4.1 | 4.2 |
| | | 2 | 4.4 | 4.3 | 4.3 | 4.3 | 4.2 | 4.3 |

# Chapter 4: Transfer of Training in Endurance Events

Over the course of the individual process of achieving sports form in every type of endurance, one or another type of specialized exercise is used. These help with developing critical physical qualities that are imperative for achieving the required level of sporting results in competition exercises. Regardless of the difference between the various types of endurance, in most cases there is a lot of overlap. This is especially true in regards to the means of developing endurance in the beginner and the undertrained athlete. In some form or fashion, athletes of all qualification will use means of developing all types of endurance (Phosphagen, glycolytic, and aerobic pathways). Only at this point, after a period of time spent training generally, should an athlete specialize and train with the goal of achieving a high level of sports results in a specific track and field event. It is unlikely that there are athletes who begin their careers training for long and ultra-long distances. At some point they all trained at medium distances and then gradually increased their training load. For example, marathoners as a rule, begin specialized running in sub-marathon, long-distance events (and achieve a high level of performance in them), and only then begin to compete in marathons. Over time, the theory and practice of physical preparation, compared to the early years, has more deeply developed the long-term preparation of runners in middle, long, and ultra-long distance running. This includes determining which means of preparation are more effective than others. It is critical to note that in the past decade more and more specialists have begun to talk about early specialization. However, even in the case of early specialization, the athlete would start out running shorter distances and progress to longer distances.

This introduction was not made by chance. We want to turn the attention of the specialist to the fact that over the course of all sports careers, athletes, regardless of the type of endurance event, use a wide variety of exercises in all three energy systems. The ratio of these depends not only on the completion of some arbitrary task, but on the specific endurance event the athlete will compete in. We assume that all energy systems, in one form or another, will play a role in increasing sports results. This helps us determine the level of transfer at various levels of long-term athletic preparation in athletes.

In Table 4.1, data are shown that demonstrate a positive transfer between competition exercises and other running exercises on various levels of sports mastery in male 800m sprinters. These data demonstrate that transfer begins with 60m runs from blocks and extends through the 3,000m run. The largest transfer was observed in the 600m and the transfer increased concomitantly with the level of sports mastery. In the 60m and 100m sprints, the higher levels of sports mastery showed a slightly higher level of transfer when compared to lower levels. According to surveys of athletes of various sports qualification, only on the two highest levels of sports mastery did the athletes use the 3,000m run. This means that the lowest correlation between the given indicators is 0.532. No athletes used the 5,000m run.

Table 4.1 – Correlation between competition results and several exercises for male 800m sprinters.

| Exercise | Sporting Result / Correlation Coefficient | | | |
|---|---|---|---|---|
| | 2.00.00 – 1.56.00 | 1.56.00 – 1.52.00 | 1.52.00 – 1.48.00 | 1.48.00 – 1.45.00 |
| 60m sprint from blocks | 0.587 | 0.602 | 0.545 | 0.456 |
| 100m sprint from blocks | 0.598 | 0.607 | 0.534 | 0.478 |
| 200m sprint from blocks | 0.632 | 0.675 | 0.655 | 0.693 |
| 400m sprint from blocks | 0.745 | 0.782 | 0.854 | 0.876 |
| 600m sprint from blocks | 0.806 | 0.886 | 0.900 | 0.924 |
| 1,000m run | 0.765 | 0.854 | 0.923 | 0.945 |
| 1,500m run | 0.600 | 0.643 | 0.743 | 0.865 |
| 3,000m run | - | - | 0.532 | 0.600 |
| 5,000m run | - | - | - | - |

In Table 4.2 the correlation coefficients between the competition distances and other running exercises for female 800m sprinters is shown. In contrast to their male counterparts, the 60 and 100m sprints only showed transfer at the two lowest levels of sports achievement. Indicators of correlational relationship fluctuate between 0.398 and 0.486. Higher transfer was observed in the 200m. Overall, there is a trend for transfer to increase as sports mastery increases. In the 1,500m, there was a slight decrease in transfer on the three highest levels of sports mastery. In the 3,000m, positive transfer was not observed at the two lowest levels of sports mastery.

Table 4.2 – Correlation between competition results and several exercises for female 800m sprinters.

| Exercise | Sporting Result / Correlation Coefficient | | | | |
|---|---|---|---|---|---|
| | 2.20.00 – 2.15.00 | 2.15.00 – 2.12.00 | 2.12.00 – 2.09.00 | 2.09.00 – 2.06.00 | 2.06.00 – 2.03.00 |
| 60m sprint from blocks | 0.456 | 0.435 | 0.398 | 0.345 | 0.365 |
| 100m sprint from blocks | 0.398 | 0.423 | 0.406 | 0.376 | 0.354 |
| 200m sprint from blocks | 0.456 | 0.534 | 0.500 | 0.600 | 0.567 |
| 400m sprint from blocks | 0.554 | 0.576 | 0.589 | 0.614 | 0.653 |
| 600m sprint from blocks | 0.776 | 0.843 | 0.878 | 0.856 | 0.923 |
| 1,000m run | 0.607 | 0.806 | 0.897 | 0.934 | 0.912 |
| 1,500m run | 0.706 | 0.645 | 0.786 | 0.876 | 0.832 |
| 3,000m run | 0.325 | 0.356 | 0.600 | 0.586 | 0.550 |
| 5,000m run | - | - | - | - | - |

Table 4.3 shows the results of correlational analysis in 1,500m runners. These numbers show that, on all levels of sports mastery, there is a positive transfer between the test indicators used and competition results. The lowest indicators of correlation between competition exercises and other running distances were in the 60, 100, 200, and 5,000m; Often, they were in the range of 0.4 – 0.5. Beginning with the 600m and ending with the 3,000m, there is an increase in the correlational relationship. Indeed, for example, in the 600m, the correlation coefficient is observed on all levels to be between 0.74 and 0.78.

Table 4.3 – Correlation between competition results and several exercises for male 1,500m runners.

| Exercise | Sporting Result / Correlation Coefficient | | | | |
|---|---|---|---|---|---|
| | 4.05.00 – 3.55.00 | 3.55.00 – 3.50.00 | 3.50.00 – 3.45.00 | 3.45.00 – 3.40.00 | 3.40.00 – 3.35.00 |
| 60m sprint from blocks | 0.398 | 0.435 | 0.400 | 0.412 | 0.409 |
| 100m sprint from blocks | 0.423 | 0.456 | 0.397 | 0.425 | 0.406 |
| 200m sprint from blocks | 0.543 | 0.500 | 0.456 | 0.508 | 0.476 |
| 400m sprint from blocks | 0.598 | 0.608 | 0.705 | 0.678 | 0.687 |
| 600m sprint from blocks | 0.789 | 0.745 | 0.785 | 0.743 | 0.786 |
| 800m sprint | 0.843 | 0.834 | 0.878 | 0.854 | 0.898 |
| 1,000m | 0.845 | 0.880 | 0.867 | 0.886 | 0.835 |
| 3,000m | 0.845 | 0.876 | 0.843 | 0.900 | 0.923 |
| 5,000m | 0.543 | 0.489 | 0.390 | 0.423 | 0.409 |
| 10,000m | - | - | - | - | - |

Table 4.4 – Correlation between competition results and several exercises for female 1,500m runners.

| Exercise | Sporting Result / Correlation Coefficient | | | | |
|---|---|---|---|---|---|
| | 4.35.00 – 4.25.00 | 4.25.00 – 4.15.00 | 4.15.00 – 4.10.00 | 4.10.00 – 4.05.00 | 4.05.00 – 4.00.00 |
| 60m sprint from blocks | 0.398 | 0.408 | 0.400 | 0.423 | 0.393 |
| 100m sprint from blocks | 0.408 | 0.412 | 0.407 | 0.435 | 0.402 |
| 200m sprint from blocks | 0.405 | 0.423 | 0.421 | 0.456 | 0.407 |
| 400m sprint from blocks | 0.500 | 0.534 | 0.543 | 0.498 | 0.567 |
| 600m sprint from blocks | 0.697 | 0.604 | 0.632 | 0.645 | 0.608 |
| 800m sprint | 0.786 | 0.765 | 0.743 | 0.779 | 0.765 |
| 1,000m | 0.800 | 0.834 | 0.888 | 0.908 | 0.914 |
| 3000m | 0.843 | 0.856 | 0.835 | 0.878 | 0.900 |
| 5000m | - | - | - | 0.453 | 0.409 |
| 10,000m | - | - | - | - | - |

Table 4.5 – Correlation between competition results and several exercises for male 5,000m runners.

| Exercise | Sporting Result / Correlation Coefficient | | | | |
|---|---|---|---|---|---|
| | 16.00.0 – 15.00.0 | 15.00.0 – 14.30.0 | 14.30.0 – 14.00.00 | 14.00.0 – 13.45.0 | 13.45.0 – 13.30.0 |
| 100m sprint from blocks | 0.332 | 0.312 | 0.344 | 0.312 | 0.345 |
| 200m sprint from blocks | 0.356 | 0.324 | 0.360 | 0.342 | 0.345 |
| 400m sprint from blocks | 0.314 | 0.367 | 0.398 | 0.453 | 0.420 |
| 600m sprint from blocks | 0.450 | 0.413 | 0.453 | 0.506 | 0.478 |
| 800m sprint | 0.600 | 0.654 | 0.602 | 0.525 | 0.543 |
| 1,000m | 0.654 | 0.678 | 0.700 | 0.734 | 0.714 |
| 3,000m | 0.786 | 0.765 | 0.798 | 0.845 | 0.900 |
| 10,000m | 0.756 | 0.784 | 0.798 | 0.908 | 0.942 |
| Half Marathon | - | - | - | - | - |

Table 4.6 – Correlation between competition results and several exercises for female 5,000m runners.

| Exercise | Sporting Result / Correlation Coefficient | | | | |
|---|---|---|---|---|---|
| | 17.00.0 – 16.30.0 | 16.30.0 – 16.00.0 | 16.00.0 – 16.30.00 | 16.30.0 – 15.30.0 | 15.30.0 – 15.00.0 |
| 100m sprint from blocks | 0.367 | 0.342 | 0.375 | 0.342 | 0.353 |
| 200m sprint from blocks | 0.317 | 0.367 | 0.345 | 0.365 | 0.354 |
| 400m sprint from blocks | 0.387 | 0.398 | 0.423 | 0.406 | 0.395 |
| 600m sprint from blocks | 0.398 | 0.423 | 0.450 | 0.465 | 0.435 |
| 800m sprint | 0.490 | 0.453 | 0.534 | 0.506 | 0.532 |
| 1,000m | 0.457 | 0.486 | 0.487 | 0.525 | 0.550 |
| 3,000m | 0.764 | 0.785 | 0.809 | 0.834 | 0.802 |
| 10,000m | 0.700 | 0.786 | 0.834 | 0.845 | 0.856 |
| Half Marathon | - | - | 0.568 | 0.608 | 0.670 |

Table 4.7 – Correlation between competition results and several exercises for male 10,000m runners.

| Exercise | Sporting Result / Correlation Coefficient | | | | |
|---|---|---|---|---|---|
| | 34.00.0 – 30.00.0 | 30.00.0 – 29.30.0 | 29.30.0 – 29.00.00 | 29.00.0 – 28.30.0 | 28.30.0 – 28.00.0 |
| 100m sprint from blocks | 0.298 | 0.324 | 0.302 | 0.297 | 0.276 |
| 200m sprint from blocks | 0.309 | 0.345 | 0.323 | 0.314 | 0.320 |
| 400m sprint from blocks | 0.354 | 0.321 | 0.345 | 0.323 | 0.333 |
| 600m sprint from blocks | 0.398 | 0.405 | 0.423 | 0.394 | 0.400 |
| 800m sprint | 0.432 | 0.420 | 0.432 | 0.396 | 0.432 |
| 1,000m | 0.425 | 0.398 | 0.423 | 0.415 | 0.456 |
| 3,000m | 0.556 | 0.576 | 0.523 | 0.587 | 0.570 |
| 5,000m | 0.776 | 0.790 | 0.845 | 0.890 | 0.876 |
| Half Marathon | - | - | - | 0.786 | 0.809 |

Table 4.8 – Correlation between competition results and several exercises for female 10,000m runners.

| Exercise | Sporting Result / Correlation Coefficient | | | | |
|---|---|---|---|---|---|
| | 40.00.0 – 34.00.0 | 34.00.0 – 33.00.0 | 33.00.0 – 32.00.00 | 32.00.0 – 31.00.0 | 31.00.0 – 30.00.0 |
| 100m sprint from blocks | 0.256 | 0.342 | 0.312 | 0.300 | 0.287 |
| 200m sprint from blocks | 0.300 | 0.288 | 0.324 | 0.303 | 0.321 |
| 400m sprint from blocks | 0.276 | 0.289 | 0.345 | 0.327 | 0.350 |
| 600m sprint from blocks | 0.345 | 0.325 | 0.340 | 0.360 | 0.350 |
| 800m sprint | 0.390 | 0.405 | 0.465 | 0.325 | 0.370 |
| 1,000m | 0.407 | 0.435 | 0.400 | 0.390 | 0.396 |
| 3,000m | 0.452 | 0.456 | 0.500 | 0.486 | 0.465 |
| 5,000m | 0.798 | 0.845 | 0.808 | 0.879 | 0.880 |
| Half Marathon | - | - | - | 0.785 | 0.874 |

Table 4.9 – Correlation between competition results and several running exercises for male 3000m runners.

| Exercise | Sporting Result / Correlation Coefficient | | | | |
|---|---|---|---|---|---|
| | 9.45.00 – 9.30.00 | 9.30.00 – 9.15.00 | 9.15.00 – 9.00.00 | 9.00.0 – 8.45.00 | 8.45.00 – 8.30.00 |
| 100m sprint from blocks | 0.278 | 0.324 | 0.307 | 0.325 | 0.354 |
| 400m sprint | 0.325 | 0.367 | 0.313 | 0.350 | 0.334 |
| 600m sprint | 0.397 | 0.445 | 0.436 | 0.486 | 0.424 |
| 800m sprint | 0.459 | 0.487 | 0.465 | 0.475 | 0.488 |
| 1,000m | 0.500 | 0.543 | 0.524 | 0.578 | 0.581 |
| 1,500m | 0.486 | 0.588 | 0.600 | 0.643 | 0.624 |
| 3,000m | 0.798 | 0.807 | 0.845 | 0.876 | 0.868 |
| 5,000m | 0.826 | 0.865 | 0.834 | 0.877 | 0.854 |
| Half Marathon | 0.666 | 0.645 | 0.689 | 0.700 | 0.676 |

Table 4.10 – Energy Supply of Muscle Work (according to V.N. Platonov, 1995)

| Source | Pathway of Synthesis | Time Required for Maximal Activation | Duration of Action | Duration of Maximal Energy Production |
|---|---|---|---|---|
| Phosphocreatine | ATP-PCr | 0s | Up to 30s | Up to 10s |
| Anaerobic Glycolytic | Glycolysis with creation of Lactate | 15-20s | 15-20s to 5-6min | From 30s to 1.5min |
| Aerobic | Oxidation of fats and carbs using $O_2$ | 90-180s | Hours | 2-5min and beyond |

An interesting note on this topic is the attention given in the literature to one or another product of the energy pathways in running events over medium and long distances (Tables 4.11 and 4.12). As shown in other data (Tables 4.1 – 4.9), in the overwhelming majority of cases, there is no positive transfer between competition results and runs of 100 and 200m. This is explained by the fact that anaerobic exercises, in large part, do not use the same energy mechanisms as aerobic exercises in either form or function.

Table 4.11 - Estimated contribution of the energy pathways in selected running events (from Greene and Pate)

| Percent Contribution to Generating ATP | | |
|---|---|---|
| Distance | Aerobic (%) | Anaerobic (%) |
| 800m* | 44 - 57 | 38 - 50 |
| 1,500m – 1 mile** | 75 - 76 | 22 - 24 |
| 3,000m | 86 - 88 | 12 - 14 |
| 5,000m | 87 - 93 | 7 - 13 |
| * Approximately 5-6% of the energy needs met by ATP-PCr<br><br>** Approximately 1-2% of the energy needs met by ATP-PCr | | |

Table 4.12
Energy production percentage in middle-distance running

| Distance | ATP - PCr (%) | Glycolysis (%) | Aerobic (%) |
|---|---|---|---|
| 800m | 10 | 30 | 60 |
| 1,500m | 8 | 20 | 72 |
| 3,000m | 5 | 15 | 80 |
| 5,000m | 4 | 10 | 86 |
| 10km | 2-3 | 8-12 | 85-90 |

# Chapter 5 – Transfer of Training in Aerobic Exercises on Glycolytic and Phosphagen Energy Systems

Beginning roughly in the 1960's, the overwhelming majority of endurance training specialists claimed that aerobic work builds a base for the development of sports results in the glycolytic and phosphagen energy systems. From this time forward, over the course of the first half of the preparation period (the stage of general preparation), it was recommended to use aerobic exercises and in the second half of preparation (the stage of special preparation), glycolytic and phosphagen system training, in addition to some maintenance of aerobic loads. The first exercises refer to the means of general preparation. In addition to these concepts, according to the stages of general preparation, the athlete must reach a given level of aerobic performance that, over the course of the next stage of realization, will help build the results in glycolytic and phosphagen exercises. From this we can infer that the glycolytic and phosphagen exercises are given a secondary role in the development of sport results. In addition, there are several works that remind us of the fact that at the conclusion of the stage of general preparation, athletes must enter a state of aerobic fitness, be it a state of sports form or some type of trainedness. Moreover, these texts do not specify what exactly constitutes a state of aerobic trainedness. In one case, there is discussion about reaching a set level of sports results in greater distance runs; in another, in several general indicators of internal load. For example, these include several metrics such as heart rate (HR), lactate threshold, $VO_2$ max (both relative and absolute), as well as HR after intense exertion (EPOC), and others. In this chapter, we are about to undertake the problem of transfer of training between aerobic indicators, Phosphagen indicators, and glycolytic indicators from the perspective of supplying skeletal muscle with energy using these three pathways.

## General Characteristics of the Aerobic System

All specialists agree that, when compared to the two other pathways, the aerobic system is the slowest activated and longest acting pathway that fuels muscle work. This is explained by the body's large capacity to store the substrates of this system (adipose tissue and glycogen) and also by the long chemical processes used to break down energy in the presence of oxygen.

The biochemical processes of aerobic energy supply can be separated into three stages. They are shown in figure 5.1.

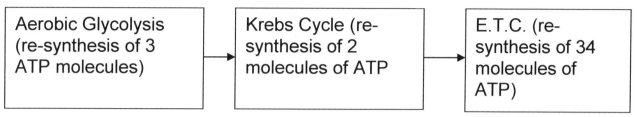

| Aerobic Glycolysis (re-synthesis of 3 ATP molecules) | → | Krebs Cycle (re-synthesis of 2 molecules of ATP | → | E.T.C. (re-synthesis of 34 molecules of ATP) |

Figure 5.1 – stages of biochemical reactions for the re-synthesis of ATP in aerobic processes.

Over the course of the first of these stages, there is a conversion of glycogen and free-fatty acids (FFA's) into acetyl CoA – a reduced form of acetic acid. This facilitates all downstream processes of energy supply in the various pathways. However, until the formation of acetyl CoA, the oxidation of glycogen and FFA occurs independently. With the aid of oxygen, 1 molecule of glycogen is completely split into carbon dioxide ($CO_2$) and water ($H_2O$), with an energy release sufficient for the re-synthesis of 39 molecules of ATP. The first stage of the aerobic process is called "aerobic glycolysis" and its by-products include ATP and $H_2O$. Here, glycogen is converted into glucose and glucose to pyruvic acid and then into ATP. In this first reaction, oxygen does not play a role.

Here we see 1 molecule of glycogen becomes two molecules of pyruvate. At the second stage of aerobic respiration, or the Kreb's Cycle, we see a series of complex biochemical reactions where a progressive exchange of electrons contributes to the re-synthesis of ATP in the electron transport chain. $CO_2$ from this stage is sent, via the blood, to the lungs where it is eliminated from the body. The Kreb's Cycle produces very little ATP itself, but is a critical component of aerobic respiration (Fig. 5.2).

During the third and final stage of aerobic respiration, the electron transport chain takes effect. Substrates from the Kreb's cycle play an integral role in converting ADP back into ATP.

In terms of efficiency, it is worthy to note that roughly 40% of the energy that comes from the oxidation of fats and carbs (primary fuel sources for aerobic respiration) goes to fuel muscular work, the rest is released as heat.

## Phosphagen System of Fueling Skeletal Muscle Contraction

I would like to remind the reader that in all three energy pathways the primary fuel source for the muscle is ATP. We are talking about the energy that will be generated after the various substrates are oxidized in the muscle. Furthermore, depending on the specifics of the action on the systems of the body the phosphagen, glycolytic, or aerobic production of ATP will become the primary source of energy for biochemical reactions. The formation of the phosphagen substrate occurs according to its various phosphate compounds. Primarily, ATP and creatine-phosphate. Phosphocreatine (PCr) is used as a substrate for energy production in sports disciplines as referenced in many texts over the course of the last decade. This is especially true for the training of athletes in speed-strength events and power-type sports. Indeed, for example the body uses PCr to more efficiently produce a high amount of force in a short amount of time. If ATP is broken down in the first seconds of high intensity work, then the PCr reaction concurrently occurs as well. The primary substrates of the phosphagen pathway are creatine (Cr) and inorganic phosphate (Pi). This process of converting energy substrates is carried out by an enzyme called creatine-phosphate, and looks like this:

Creatine kinase
CrP -----------------------→ Cr + P $_{,,}$ + energy

Energy fuels the reduction of Cr and Pi back into ATP. ATP is then oxidized to form ADP and another Pi. In order to re-synthesize PCr, only energy released by the oxidation of ATP can be used. The re-synthesis of PCr comes after the re-synthesis of ATP. Here, stores of PCr cannot be held at maximal capacity while executing training loads. However, it is possible to restore them during a period of rest after a high intensity bout of exercise.

Another detail about the phosphagen system is that it only acts for a very brief moment; its duration of action is relatively brief. It can be activated quite rapidly, within seconds. However, after 10 seconds or so, its maximal output is exhausted and its fueling effect begins to wane. The rate of power development within the phosphagen system depends on the amount of phosphate in the muscle. According to data from Spriet, et. al. (1999) rapid muscle contractions deplete PCr 10-15% faster than slow contractions. A similar concentration of ATP is observed in muscle regardless of type of muscle contraction. The rate of the phosphocreatine reaction is affected by other factors as well. For example, with an increase in sports qualification, there is a parallel increase in PCr in the muscle fibers; up to 70% greater as compared to muscles in un-trained athletes (N. I. Volkov, 2000). As sports results increase in the short sprints, there is a higher efficiency for oxidizing phosphate compounds (Hirvonen et. al,

1987). In terms of increasing the duration of the training effect in the yearly cycle of training (months), we see an increase in phosphate reduction (ATP and Cr) in muscle fibers of weightlifters (Spriet, 1999). Here we see that the issue is centered around the development of sports form and we observe that not only increases in the rate of energy mobilization but also the oxidation of phosphate bonds (adaption reaction) affect the development of sports form. It is quite obvious that the rate of the phosphocreatine reaction, according to phosphate compound reduction, depends on the activity of various enzymes (Yakovlev, N. N., 1974. Kots, M.Y., 1986).

## General Characteristics of the Glycolytic Pathway

In this system of energy supply, in contrast to the aerobic and phosphocreatine systems, re-synthesis of ATP in the muscles occurs as a result of glucose or glycogen oxidation without oxygen. This reaction, as referenced in the literature, has been referred to as "anaerobic glycolysis." These reactions utilize glucose in the blood. It is specific in the fact that it utilizes a complete splitting of the glucose molecule. As ATP accumulates, a by-product called lactate begins to accumulate as well.

In contrast to the phosphocreatine chemical reactions, the glycolytic biochemical process is more complex. In the beginning, glucose or glycogen molecules are reduced to lactate, which is later used to re-synthesize ATP (Fig. 5.3). The initial and rapid reaction of the glycolytic pathway is due to the activity of a variety of enzymes. It is important to note that the speed of the glycolytic reaction is quite rapid. It creates a large amount of energy due to the intense expenditure of glycogen. In contrast to the phosphocreatine system, which is at maximal energy output within seconds, the glycolytic system is at peak production much later. According to the literature, reaching maximal output takes 20-25 seconds. At this point, the glycolytic system is the primary driver for the energy supply of working muscles. Under prolonged, high intensity and glycolytic loads, the aforementioned factors (time to max output and duration of effect) should be taken into consideration.

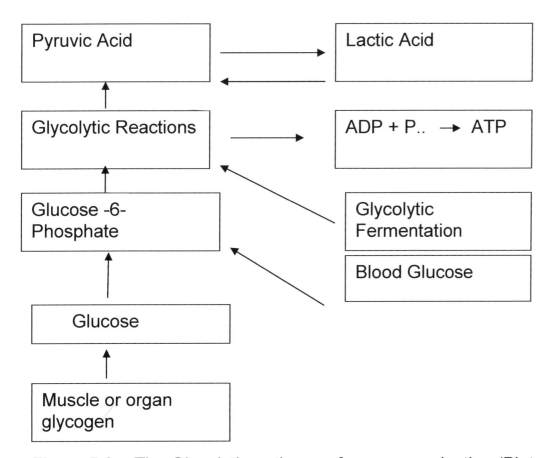

Figure 5.3 – The Glycolytic pathway of energy production (Platonov, 2005).

# Transfer of Training Between the Various Energy Supply Systems

We will begin with the question of the aerobic mechanism of energy supply in running, for various distances (Fig. 5.4). First, it is obvious that a 100m sprint will not use the aerobic system at all. In a 200m sprint however, it will contribute roughly 10% of the energy supply. In longer distances, the role of the aerobic system will increase concomitantly with the increase in distance. It takes over nearly all of the energy supply to working muscles at distances of 5,000m and beyond.

As shown in Figure 5.5, there is a decrease in the amount of aerobic contribution as the contribution of anaerobic energy supply goes up. If we compare the material in both figures, then it becomes clear that there is absolutely no way that the aerobic system can contribute to an increase in sporting results for the 100 and 200m sprints. The same argument could be made for up to 400m sprints.

Unfortunately, in the theory and practice of physical preparation, there is an acute lack of work which focuses on the degree of transfer of the aerobic energy supply on the phosphocreatine and glycolytic pathways. We see that in high intensity exercise it plays almost zero role, and starts to slowly contribute at around 400m. To a certain degree, this is demonstrated in Table 5.1 which shows the percent of each energy system's contribution to the re-synthesis of ATP in runs of various intensities and distances, as well as the type of muscular work, as shown in Table 5.2.

In Table 5.3, we see the contributors to fueling muscular work in the three different pathways. This material demonstrates the fact that the pathway, time, and mode of muscle work all play roles in the duration and maximal effect that each of the various energy systems has on the body.

All three are fundamentally different; they have very little overlap in terms of sports performance. All of these things speak to the fact that transfer of training, in terms of fueling muscular work, in principle, cannot exist. Exceptions here may include the phosphocreatine and glycolytic systems, in some cases, such as in the 200m or even 400m sprints. This phenomenon is never observed in runs of greater distances. Under this high intensity type of muscular work, there is not one type of energy provided, but several. It is true that the various substrates of energy production differ (Fig. 5.6). We are referring to the way that they overlap within a working muscle over time (Tables 5.1-5.2). They dictate the specifics of each type of run over short, medium, and long distances as well as the different types of muscular contractions during the training process. This is particularly pertinent in interval running, where the anaerobic and aerobic process both take part in fueling exercise.

Take another example of the correlational relationship between energy systems in the 400m, 800m, 1,500m, 10,000m, and marathon from Table 5.3. According to the increase in distance from 400m up to 10,000m, we observe an increase in the ratio of aerobic contribution and a decrease in the other systems contribution to fueling muscle work. At marathon distances, aerobic energy is derived from roughly 40% fats and 60% carbohydrates.

In my view here, for the running events that contain similar energy demands by nature, there could exist some degree of positive transfer. Of course, the more these elements overlap, the greater degree of transfer will exist. Similarly, when looking at the question of transfer between aerobic exercises on anaerobic exercises it is critical to bear in mind that the aerobic pathway is the primary fuel source for extensive or longer distance work. From this we can say that the greatest coefficient of correlation will be between runs of longer distances. In terms of shorter runs and sprints, the transfer of training will be greater from phosphocreatine and glycolytic exercises.

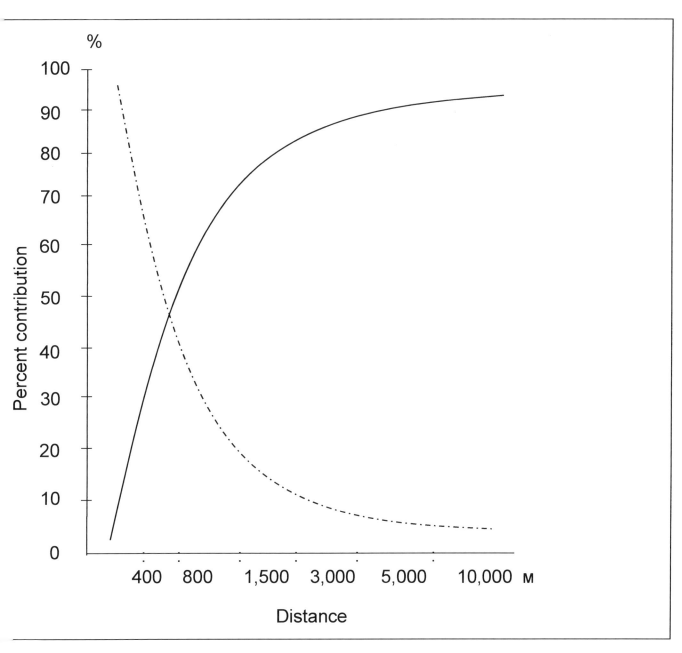

Figure 6.6 – Ratio of anaerobic (-----) and aerobic ( - ) pathways for energy supply in runs of various distances (according to V.N. Platonov, 1986).

Table 5.1 –Percent contribution of various sources of energy in re-synthesizing ATP for various types of running (according to Newsheiome et.al. 1992).

| Type of Run | Percent Contribution in Re-Synthesis of ATP | | | | |
| | CRF | Glycogen | | Blood Glucose (liver Glycogen) | Lactate (from fat) |
| | | anaerobic | aerobic | | |
|---|---|---|---|---|---|
| 100 | 50 | 50 | - | - | - |
| 200 | 25 | 62 | 10 | - | - |
| 400 | 12.5 | 62.5 | 25 | - | - |
| 800 | - | 50 | 50 | - | - |
| 1,500m | - | 25 | 75 | - | - |
| 5,000m | - | 12.5 | 87.5 | - | - |
| 10,000m | - | 3 | 97 | - | - |
| Marathon | - | - | 75 | 5 | 20 |

Table 5.2 –Sources of energy supply for muscular work (according to V.N.Platonov, 1986).

| Energy Source | Source of Supply | Time for Activation | Duration of Effect | Duration of Maximal Energy Supply |
|---|---|---|---|---|
| Anaerobic Alactic | ATP - PCr | 0 sec. | Up to 30 sec. | Up to 10 sec. |
| Lactic | Glycolysis and lactate | 15-20 sec. | 30 sec. – 6 min. | 30 – 90 sec. |
| Aerobic | Aerobic respiration using carbs and fats | 90 sec. – 3 min. | Hours | 2-5 min. |

Table 5.3 – Ratio of various pathways for muscular energy supply in 400m, 800m, 1.5k, 10k, and marathon runs (from data by N.I. Volkova et. al. 2000).

| Distance | Ratio of Energy Supply |
|---|---|
| 400m | Aerobic (carbohydrate) ~5%<br>Glycolysis ~75%<br>PCr ~20% |
| 800m | Aerobic (carbohydrate) ~45%<br>Glycolysis ~53%<br>PCr ~2% |
| 1,500m | Aerobic (carbohydrate) ~60%<br>Glycolysis ~38%<br>PCr ~2% |
| 10,000m | Aerobic (carbohydrate) ~90%<br>Glycolysis ~9%<br>PCr ~1% |
| Marathon | Aerobic from carbohydrate ~40%<br>Aerobic from fats ~60% |

Table 5.4 – Average values for maximal consumption of oxygen in runners of elite qualification in various distances (according to Svedenhag, Sjodin, 1994)

| Distance | Vo2 Max (ml/kg/min) |
|---|---|
| 400m | 63 |
| 800m | 69 |
| 800 - 1,500m | 73 |
| 1,500 - 5,000m | 75 |
| 5,000 - 10,000m | 85 |
| Marathon | 73 |

# Chapter 6 – Transfer of Training in Speed-Strength Events of Track and Field

## With a specific emphasis on the connection between slow and fast twitch muscle function

I have already briefly touched on this topic in the foreword. Specifically, the fact that fast and slow twitch muscles are so-named because they contain fibers that contract fast and slow, respectively.

Before we examine the problem of transfer between these two types of muscle fibers and their function in various exercises, let's first examine their function. In the theory and practice of physical preparation, in accordance with the data available from many areas of scientific research (anatomy and physiology, specifically), it is quite clear that the muscular system of humans (as in all warm-blooded mammals) is comprised of two types of muscle fibers: slow and fast twitch. The first of these is primarily responsible for slow movements and the second, fast movements. Secondly, each individual has a unique composition of fast and slow twitch fibers based on genetic predisposition. This composition remains relatively constant over the course of a person's life and cannot be changed much based on any type of training. Under the influence of physical training, the cross sectional diameter of the fiber can be increased, as seen with weight lifting. This clarifies the conclusion that sports results in any type of athletic endeavor are largely determined genetically, based on the predisposed ratio of slow to fast twitch fibers. For example, in sprinters a higher amount of fast twitch muscle predisposes an athlete to a better result. In endurance athletes, not so much.

This ratio can be quite varied: For example, an athlete could have 70 percent fast twitch and 30 percent slow twitch or a 50-50 split. Many variations are common based on genetic predisposition. Of course, in the process of completing isometric exercises, the amplitude of contractions in fast and slow muscle is equally high. In dynamic exercises however, the amplitude can vary up or down in the respective fibers.

Now let us discuss the question of the transfer between these two types of muscle fibers in completing various physical exercises. In the literature, as well as in the theory and practice of physical preparation, having compiled the knowledge from various pertinent scientific disciplines in biology and kinesiology, I have not discovered a single location where the essence of this issue has been enlightened for us. The knowledge of the mechanisms of work for slow and fast twitch muscle fibers can help specialists in the theory and practice of physical preparation discern what is needed in the process of individual training programs as well as the understanding of transfer of training in various types of sport.

I will present my ideas on the mechanisms of transfer between slow and fast twitch muscle in the process of executing various exercises. In order to do this in the most efficient way I will draw on decades of research and other coaches experiences in the world of athletics. First and foremost, we will cover the development of maximal speed and maximal strength and of course the mechanisms of their training in speed-strength types of sport (primarily in track and field). In the experiences of many coaches it becomes clear that slow, as with fast twitch muscle fibers, have their own recruitment threshold in speed and strength.

It is likely that slow twitch muscle fibers contribute more to maximal strength movements than to maximal speed movements. For example, in the process of performing strength exercises with maximal or supramaximal intensities (95% - 120%) the contractile velocity of the limb is slow and the duration of the contraction is comparatively long. In contrast, dynamic exercises (lower intensities, from 5% - 20% for example) have a high contractile velocity and the duration of the action is relatively short. Therefore, fast twitch fibers will contribute more in this case than the slow twitch fibers. It follows that in the first case, the athlete reaches a near maximal or supramaximal level of development in strength qualities, and not in speed qualities. On the other hand, when a maximal speed contraction is observed, there is a greater development of maximal speed qualities, as compared to maximal strength qualities.

Here it is important to note that slow twitch fibers can be activated with fast twitch fibers, when a sufficient load is placed upon them for a sufficient amount of time. This idea of threshold velocity of activation is explained by Henneman's size principle. Note that there are two qualifications for the slow twitch fibers to activate under high intensity loads: large stimulus and long duration of action. These constraints are biological in nature, as ST fibers cannot fully activate in a short period of time. Here in lies one reason for the difference in strength and speed qualities in the respective fibers. For example, in the process of performing the bench press on an incline, or the full squat, where the athlete is lifting near maximal or supramaximal intensity, the athlete develops speed at much less than 1 meter per second (m/s), whereas in exercises such as the snatch, using 10-20% of maximum, the barbell can reach much greater velocities. So, when using maximal intensities, maximal strength is the primary adaptation and in faster movements, maximal speed is the primary adaptation. Here it is critical to remember the facts: the theory and practice of physical preparation testifies to the point that increasing global muscle activation, which concomitantly grows as external resistance is increased, decreases the display of speed qualities. Practically used in the training process, these types of loads can increase maximal strength while using lighter loads will increase maximal speed. Max strength develops using moderate and high zones of intensity (% of 1RM in weightlifting). When developing maximal speed, lower zones of intensity are used but also exercises are selected where high velocities can be attained. This will recruit fast twitch muscle fibers. In both cases, we are talking about improving strength and speed qualities using various weightlifting means.

Now, on the other hand, take for example the use of exercises without external resistance. If you are moving very rapidly (90-95% of max speed), you are operating at a high intensity but will be recruiting mostly fast twitch fibers, whereas if you are using low intensity (slower speed) you will be recruiting more slow-twitch fibers. It is critical to note that in the process of developing maximal strength and maximal speed there are several levels of intensity used in the various exercises (zones of intensity), after which point the body is recruiting primarily one type of muscle fiber (fast or slow). Of course, it is critical to designate each zone of intensity. For example, in weightlifting, it is entirely possible that both fast and slow twitch fibers are moving weight over 90 percent of max (even as low as 80-85%).

In the process of developing maximal speed, it is entirely possible that this requires the use of training loads under 50% of max. Here we are talking about (again) those exercises with a barbell. Naturally, in the first example, the exercises using the most speed will be with lower intensities and the ones with higher intensities will be at a lower speed, recruiting more slow twitch fibers.

As intensity goes up, larger amounts of slow twitch fibers will be required (in addition to fast twitch fibers) to perform maximal contractions. This unique mode of work is most specific to weightlifting. For example, weightlifters use high intensities (80% to over 100% of max).

Fast twitch fibers are the primary movers for exercises completed at high velocities. What I mean here is that zones of intensity (speed being the load) over 80% of max will largely recruit fast twitch fibers. These exercises are used in many general track and field disciplines, with external resistance or with external assistance.

Using isometric exercises, regardless of their duration or zone of intensity (could be low, medium, or high intensity), slow twitch fibers are almost always taking part. In difficult motor coordination tasks and exercises, as well as in those exercises where several joints take part, slow and fast twitch muscle mass can take part in turn. In one part of a movement, slow twitch may be the primary driver, and in another – fast twitch. This complex interplay is natural and ultimately specific to each movement. The roles of the two types of fibers depend in large part on the speed of the load being moved. High velocity movements will recruit more fast-twitch fibers and slower movements – slow twitch. When a movement begins to slow down and become less intense, the fast twitch fibers will be recruited less and less, thus the interplay between the two types of muscle facilitates the many complex dynamics of both sport movements. This shift to slow-twitch dominance can also occur when the contractions last for a long time, as naturally prolonged muscle work will fatigue the muscle, and fast twitch fibers will fatigue much more rapidly than slow twitch fibers. For example, let us look at a few situations in weightlifting, we will begin with the full snatch. Here, in the first part of the exercise (the pull from the floor to about mid-thigh) all muscle fibers of the back and legs will perform most of the work, after this the fast twitch fibers will take over to move the lifter rapidly under the bar. This progression from slow twitch to fast twitch muscle mass is also observed in the clean, in the shot throw forward, upwards, and backwards, as well as in clean and snatch pulls. It follows that in principle, slow twitch fibers cannot develop maximal speed (in reference to transfer of training). In the same way, maximal strength and maximal speed occur independent of one another, for the most part. One may influence the other up to a certain point, or to a level of sports mastery. Allow me to clarify: maximal strength is important. Every athlete must achieve a certain level of maximal strength to enable them to build maximal speed and overall sports performance. But this is only true up to a certain point; a point at which training maximal strength begins to make the athlete slower, over-developing the slow twitch fibers and detracting from speed training.

Now, with this in mind, it is a good time to talk about starting strength (the beginning movement of any exercise), which up to a certain level is performed by all the muscle fibers. Bearing all of this in mind, it is obvious that athletes are capable of reaching one or another level of sports results having various levels of maximal strength (which can vary by 10% or more). It follows that at each consecutive level of sports achievement in competition exercises, the athlete must have a sufficient (not excessive) level of maximal strength development, which will facilitate the transfer to the concomitant level of maximal speed development. Slow twitch muscles, or groups of muscles (working together as common agonists), are recruited in exercises using light, moderate, and maximal intensities. There is a threshold velocity where fast twitch fibers are the only muscle fibers being recruited, meaning that the duration of the action is so brief that the slow twitch fibers are not activated. Given that this is a true fact, it is quite apparent that the specific development of maximal strength and the specific development maximal speed occurs independently. It follows that to carry out a specific developmental exercise we can select which adaptation to target: maximal strength development or maximal speed development, based on objective criteria.

For developing maximal speed we must ensure that the movement is carried out with great speed, regardless of load (be it light, moderate, maximal, or supramaximal). Allow me to explain what I mean when I refer to load in the context of developing the fast twitch fibers. Exercises carried out at high velocities can be done in resisted or assisted conditions without external load (barbell, sleds, or other implements) for example a sprint uphill or a sprint downhill. They can also be performed with an external load, such as, for example, a barbell snatch using 20-30% of the athlete's max.

When developing one or another of these qualities, three different types of exercises can be used. Exercise type one: coaches can utilize exercises that exclusively target one or the other adaptation. For example, developing the maximal strength of the legs only (for example, squats at

90-95% of max) or only the maximal speed of the legs (for example, 30-60m sprints from a standing start).

Exercise type two: coaches can target a mixture of slow and fast twitch characteristics, slow first and then fast. These types of exercises are things like cleans from the floor with a light load. The first pull is focused primarily on strength, whereas the rest of the lift (above the knee) targets speed.

Exercise type three relates to those movements that use speed to start, then strength, and then speed again. This recruitment interplay of fast and slow twitch fibers can also go strength, speed, strength. Let's take a look at an example of the first scenario. When holding the bar on the back, preparing to perform the snatch catch, the athlete will bend the knees, then drive the bar and rapidly drop down to catch it overhead. Again, at the point of the catch, the athlete is using strength to overcome their inertia with the added load of the bar, reverse the load and stand up.

Now we will look at an example of the second variation: speed, strength, speed. For this case, we will use the long jump. During the first phase (running start) speed is the primary driver. When the plant leg hits the board, strength (maximal as well as isometric) functions to reverse the athletes weight and support the body. As the drive leg pushes through, fast twitch muscles are activated again and the athlete takes flight over the pit. A similar recruitment profile is observed in the depth jump to broad jump.

In the training process, maximal strength characteristics can be accomplished using similar exercises to those that develop speed. For example, to develop maximal strength in the upper body, use the bench press at 90-95% of maximum. For developing speed of the arms, use a shot put at competition and lighter implement weights. Or, a coach could use a bench press at 30-50% of maximum intensity. In the first case (high intensity) the bar speed will be much lower than 1 m/s, and in the second it will be much faster. From the second example, it follows that if too high of a load is used, the speed attained in the bench press will not be fast enough to elicit a maximal speed adaptation.  Again, it is important to note that there is very little transfer between the qualities of these two maximal characteristics. In some cases they contribute to the performance of certain movements by working in turn at different stages of the movement, but this does not constitute a direct transfer of training means.

In addition to the information above, I would also add the experimental material (compiled from various peer reviewed sources), that has examined the properties of slow and fast (two sub-types) twitch muscle mass relative to their use in sports performance (Table 6.1).

Table 6.1 – Several means of slow and fast muscle (two sub-types) fibers that play a role in the process of developing sports form.

| Action of Muscle Fiber | Type of Muscle Fiber | | |
| --- | --- | --- | --- |
| | Slow Twitch | Fast Twitch | |
| | | Sub-Type A | Sub-Type X |
| Speed of Contraction | Slow | Fast | Fast |
| Contribution to Hypertrophy | High | Small | Small |
| Rate of Fatigue | Low | High | Very High |
| Power | Low | High | Very High |
| Degree of Mitochondrial Activity | Very High | High | Low |
| Energy Source | Fat | Creatine - Phosphate | Creatine-Phosphate |

Again, we see that the assertion of the influence of maximal strength (A. Hill, 1938-1949) or maximal dynamic strength (Y.V. Verkhoshanksy, 1978) on maximal speed is, at its core, flawed. In the first case, one can only utilize the adapted dynamic strength when transitioning into a high velocity movement, at which point it no longer contributes to sporting results. For example, in track and field sprints, take the amortization phase beginning at the moment of foot contact with the ground after the flight phase and remaining there (thousandths of a second) up until the full extension of the hip, knee, and ankle joints. In the long jump, the dynamic strength of the leg plays a role not only in the approach, but also in the moment of pre-launch, when the foot is placed on the board, up until the athlete takes off. Here there is a required level of a certain amount of both static, dynamic, and maximal strength to perform exercises which require a reversal of the athletes mass, as well as the mass of an implement. In the first case, we will look at the high jump. Here the athlete's jump is a result of the rotational action of the plant leg, in the moment that it stops the forward motion of the athlete and transfers it vertically. For the plant leg (under isometric load) to avoid losing torque in the horizontal plane, it must bend somewhat at the knee. In track and field, in practically all of its forms, isometric strength interacts with dynamic strength. This means that in the interplay between isometric and dynamic modes of work, the isometric contraction plays a role in facilitating the dynamic contraction, as with the bent knee of the high jumper. If this is indeed true, then the athlete must obtain a sufficient level of static *and* dynamic strength. We constantly talk about a "sufficient level" of strength, but not a maximal level. The given experimental material in the first three chapters of this book demonstrate that athletes on all levels of sports mastery corroborate this finding, that "sufficient" is true rather than "maximal" in regards to strength. This understanding of the issue explains why athletes who have the same level of sports results in competition exercises, can have totally different levels in various strength test indicator exercises.

# Chapter 7 – Transfer Process of Developing Sports Form Using A Variety of Exercises

As we begin this final chapter, I would like to point out to the reader one subtle, but crucial detail. This chapter is not about the transfer between exercises, but transfer in the process of developing sports form. Allow me to clarify: here we are talking about the use of a complex of exercises that will cause the athletes to enter sports form in certain exercises or movements *not being used* during that cycle of training. This is a phenomenon based on transfer between physiological qualities, biomechanics, and exercise selection. Clearly, the process of entering into a state of sports form is organically connected with sacrificing some long-term adaptations, to a certain extent. However, both short and long term adaptations are a consequence of the effect of a certain system of training loads utilized during the periods of development of sports form. Practically speaking, we as coaches are the witnesses of the existence of a relationship between pedagogical and biological processes; they simultaneously constitute the entry into sports form. Both of these, at their core, describe the whole idea behind what we are talking about here.

**Transfer between exercises being used in a block of training and exercises not being used**

How do we begin the transfer process of developing sports form in exercises not currently being used in a given period of training? For this, it is foundational, at the moment of entry into sports form in a given set of exercises, to identify a set level of results in test exercises that will not be used over the next period of developing sports form. After the conclusion of long-term sports research (primarily from coaches and athletes specializing in speed strength events of track and field) we have compiled results that demonstrate several principles of transfer in the process of developing sports form in exercises that are not being used in the current period of training. In a search of the experimental data (questioning athletes and coaches) we were met with several obstacles. Rarely did athletes use, over the course of developing sports form, one or another of these exercises. More often than not, the training programs used a variation of several similar exercises in form and in function. This primarily includes running exercises (hurdles, 400m hurdles, and medium distance runs). For example, in sprints, for most athletes, jumping and short distance runs are used. In one case, middle distance sprinters, long distance runners, and ultra-long distance runners used one or another exercise over the course of the period of developing sports form. Practically, in several cases, we ran into non-traditional means of constructing periods of developing sports form. In these cases, the athletes, for some reason (most likely being forced), used only one exercise.

We will start with the sprints, where the athletes generally use short sprints for developing maximal speed and longer distances for developing speed endurance. In our case, one group of athletes used, over the course of developing sports form, only short sprints (and hurdles) – 60m. A second group only used 150m sprints, a third only 200m, a fourth only 300m, and a fifth only 500m. The data we received for this group of sprinters is shown in Table 7.1.

Table 7.1 – Transfer of exercises that were "used" during a training cycle onto exercises that were "not used" in groups of hurdlers.

| Used | Un-used |
|---|---|
| 60m sprints from blocks and standing start | 60m hurdles from blocks and standing start, 100m sprints, broad jumps, and 60m hill sprints |
| 150m sprints from standing start | 60, 100, 200m sprints, 60m hurdles, 100 and 110m sprints from blocks, broad jumps |
| 60m hurdles from blocks and standing start | 60 and 100m sprints from blocks and standing start, 100m hurdles and 110m hurdles, broad jumps |
| 200m sprints from blocks and standing start | 60, 100, 150 and 300m sprints from blocks and standing start, broad jumps |
| 300m from blocks or standing start | 100, 150, 200, and 400m sprints, 400m hurdles |
| 500m from a standing start | 400m hurdles, 200, 300, 400, and 600m sprints |

Table 7.2 shows the results of experimental data for the respondent jumping athletes, which, for various reasons, include only competition and strength exercises over the course of the periods of developing sports form.

In contrast to the sprints and jumps groups, throwers more often used various implement weights. Results of the transfer process are shown in Table 7.3. We should pay special attention to the experimental data from runners over various distances and throwers in the process of which we observed significant transfer to strength and jumping exercises (Table 7.4). Most of these, other than the bench press, were used in all sprints, jumps, and throwing events. This is what interests us, particularly about these events in track and field.

Table 7.2 – Transfer process of developing sports form with used exercises compared to un-used exercises in groups of jumpers

| Used | Un-used |
|---|---|
| Broad Jumps | 60m sprints from blocks, vertical jumps, triple jumps |
| High Jumps | Broad jumps |
| Triple Jumps | Broad and high jumps, 60m sprints with low and standing start |
| Pole Vault | 60m sprints low and standing start, broad and high jumps, 60m hurdles low and standing start |

Table 7.3 – Transfer process of developing sports form in un-used exercises by using a complex of exercises.

| Used Exercise | Improvement in Un-Used Exercises. |
|---|---|
| Shot toss (throw with both hands) | ± 7 – 10% (Hammer Throw) |
| Shot throw with a turn | ± 7 – 10% (Discus Throw) |
| Discus throw | ± 15 – 20% (Shot throw w/turn) |
| Hammer throw | ± 7 – 10% (Shot Toss) |
| Javelin throw | ± 20 – 25% (Discus Throw) |

Table 7.4 – Transfer process of developing sports form in used training exercises paired with accessory exercises that are not-used for speed-strength types of sports.

| Used Exercises | Un-Used Exercises |
|---|---|
| Snatch | Clean, floor pulls (snatch/clean), block pulls, hang pulls, shot throw forward and backward |
| Clean | Snatch pull, snatch and clean pull from the floor |
| Barbell Bench Press | Incline bench press, Standing press behind the head, pin press |
| Half Squat (back) | Half squat (front), vertical jump, standing broad jump, standing start triple jump |
| Standing Broad Jump | Vertical jump, standing start triple jump |
| Jumps 30-50m (extensive) | Vertical jump, standing broad jump, three and five fold jump from standing start |
| Standing Start Triple Jump | Vertical jump, standing broad jump, five fold jump from standing start |
| Standing Start Five Fold Jumps | Vertical jump, standing broad jump, three fold jump from standing start |

## Developing Sports Form Using Special Developmental Exercises

In this training situation, we are going to judge the process of transfer of sports form according to the number of training sessions that will be carried out over the course of periods of developing sports form using exercises similar in form and function to our test exercise. This will be done within a one training session per-day template. In the first case, over the course of periods of developing sports form, two programs will be used in rotation, which will use different exercises. In the second case, there will be three programs used in rotation. I would also like to note here that the process of developing sports form is entirely individual according to its duration. In all cases the athletes must carry out their specific, individual number of training sessions according to which they will enter into a state of sports form. In the process of experimental design and observation, we have set up 8 groups of athletes who enter sports form after a given number of training sessions. They are as follows:

First – 36 sessions

Second – 50 sessions

Third – 75 sessions

Fourth – 100 sessions

Fifth – 125 sessions

Sixth – 150 sessions

Seventh – 175 sessions

Eighth – 200 sessions

We will start by looking at the transfer process of developing sports form in the case of using two programs in rotation. Here we expect, at the end of the transfer process, that the athlete will have completed the same number of training sessions. For example, they would use the first and second programs for 18 sessions each. Here we are talking about athletes who should enter sports form after 36 sessions. For the second level of experimental data, the dynamics of transfer changes for the development of sports form in cases where athletes used, not two different programs, but three. Here we also observe indicators that the critical individual accumulation of training volume is strongly correlated to entry into sports form. For example, entry into sports form ends at the exact moment when an athlete completes 12 training sessions of any given program. Here, the overall accumulation of volume will reach 36 training sessions when the athlete (one of a group of athletes) enters into a state of sports form.

I also point out that each of the programs were selected in such a way that during their use, exercises were used that promote the transfer of sports form between developmental exercises.

In Table 7.5, we see several variations for rotation of the two different programs in groups of sprinters where, over the course of the first period, competition exercises, or highly similar exercises, were used. Here, the number of training sessions used in one exercise complements the number of sessions using other exercises. It is of great importance to note that solving the question of developing maximal speed, using maximal and supramaximal zones of intensity (as some specialists recommend), requires rest intervals of 3 – 5 minutes. When running longer distances, we can develop speed endurance. Training loads in the 80-85% range with rest periods from 1 – 2 minutes, depending on the distance sprinted, will be required for this type of adaptation.

Table 7.5 – Several competition exercises and their analogues used in the transfer process of developing sports form in groups of sprinters. These are presented in a two training program variation.

| Competition Exercises and their analogues being used | |
|---|---|
| First Variation | Second Variation |
| 60m sprints from blocks or standing | 60m hurdles from blocks or standing |
| 60m sprints from blocks or standing | 150m sprints from blocks or standing |
| 200m sprints from blocks or standing | 300m sprints from blocks or standing |
| 60m hurdles from blocks or standing | 100m sprints from blocks or standing |
| 500m sprints from blocks or standing | 600m sprints from blocks or standing |
| 100m sprints or 110m hurdles from blocks or standing | 150m sprints from blocks or standing |
| 100m sprints from blocks or standing | 200m sprints from blocks or standing |
| 300m sprints from blocks or standing | 150m sprints from blocks or standing |

The experimental data analyzed demonstrates that all athletes entered a state of sports form in every exercise according to an individual number of training sessions. Their sum is the total number of various training sessions over the course of which various training programs were used. If there were outliers, the difference was only a few training sessions. This demonstrates the transfer process of developing sports form in cases where two training programs are used (that switch off over the period of developing sports form), which are similar in form and function to one another. I would also point out that in an addition, in the 2000's, we arrived at the conclusion that glycolytic exercises facilitate the process of entry into sports form in phosphagen exercises. In this case, we are talking about training sessions that over the course of which glycolytic exercises are used, adding to an important number for overall volume of training which will cause the athlete to enter into sports form in phosphagen exercises. This relationship between the two types of exercises can be varied. An example can be constructed using two phosphagen and three glycolytic training sessions per week. For example, take the given structure of weekly cycles of training a group of athletes that enter into a state of sports form in 48 training sessions in Phosphagen exercises in 8.5 weeks. Over the course of these sessions, athletes will complete 19 Phosphagen training sessions and 29 glycolytic. The entry into sports form occurs faster in phosphagen exercises due to the transfer of the process of entry into sports form.

Transfer in the development of sports form in groups of jumpers has it's own nuances (Table 7.6). Here we observe positive transfer of training not only between jumps but also sprints (with and without hurdles). Most often, the transfer process of developing sports form with running exercises (60m sprints and hurdles, 100m sprints and hurdles) was observed in broad jumps. Positive transfer was also observed between jumps in series, broad jumps, and vertical jumps. We were able to obtain training data that demonstrate the fact that over the course of periods of developing sports form, athletes could do no broad jumping at all and still enter into sports form in given types of jumps when doing the following types of exercises: 60 and 100m sprints from blocks and standing starts, 60, 100, and 110m hurdles, pole vault, and repeated jumps in series. The relationship between these means of training can be quite varied.

Table 7.6 – Competition exercises and their analogues used in the transfer process of developing sports form in groups of jumpers. These are presented in a two training program variation. An athlete or coach would pick one of these.

| Competition Exercises and their analogues being used | |
|---|---|
| First Variation | Second Variation |
| 60m sprints from blocks or standing | Broad jumps |
| 60m sprints from blocks or standing | Broad jumps |
| Broad jumps | Vertical jumps |
| Pole vault | Broad jumps |
| Pole Vault | Vertical jumps |
| Jumping (extensive) | Broad jumps |
| Jumping (extensive) | Triple jump |
| 100m sprint | Broad jumps |
| 100m sprint and 110m hurdles from blocks or standing | Broad jumps |

Tables 7.7 – 7.8 show the results of training that relate to throws in track and field. Here, the transfer process of developing sports form was observed only in cases where the difference between the mass of the implement and the competition mass was between 7 – 20%. The largest

difference in terms of percent correlation was observed in the discus and the javelin. Here as well as in track and field jumping events, athletes can use one implement during a development cycle and enter into sports form in an implement of similar weight as well. For example, hammer throwers who use only an implement of 7.26kg will enter into sports form for implements from 6.5kg to 8kg.

Table 7.7 – Competition exercises and their analogues used in the transfer process of developing sports form in groups of throws (hammer and shot). These are presented in a two training program variation. An athlete or coach would pick one of these.

| Competition Exercises and their analogues being used | |
| --- | --- |
| First Variation | Second Variation |
| Hammer and shot throw 7.26kg | Hammer and shot throw 6.5 or 8kg |
| Hammer and shot throw 8kg | Hammer and shot throw 7.27 or 8.7kg |
| Hammer and shot throw 9kg | Hammer and shot throw 8.2 or 9.8kg |
| Hammer and shot throw 10kg | Hammer and shot throw 9 or 11kg |
| Hammer and shot throw 6kg | Hammer and shot throw 5.5 or 6.5kg |
| Hammer and shot throw 5kg | Hammer and shot throw 4.5 or 5.4kg |
| Hammer and shot throw 4kg | Hammer and shot throw 3.6 or 4.3kg |
| Hammer and shot throw 3kg | Hammer and shot throw 2.7 or 3.25kg |

Table 7.8 – Competition exercises and their analogues used in the transfer process of developing sports form in groups of throwers (disc and javelin). These are presented in a two training program variation. An athlete or coach would pick one of these.

| Competition Exercises and their analogues being used | |
|---|---|
| First Variation | Second Variation |
| Discus throw 2kg | Discus throw 2.4 or 1.7 kg |
| Discus throw 1.75kg | Discus throw 2.2 or 1.5kg |
| Discus throw 1.5kg | Discus throw 1.1 or 1.8kg |
| Discus throw and javelin 1kg | Discus throw or javelin 0.8 or 1.2kg |
| Discus throw and javelin 0.8kg | Discus throw and javelin 0.6 and 0.9kg |
| Discus throw and javelin 0.6kg | Discus throw and javelin 0.5 and 0.7kg |

Transfer of the process of developing sports form with one set of exercises (differing in duration of use) on another set of runs over middle distances and long distances has it's own specifics as well (Table 7.9). If we are talking about the development of glycolytic qualities, then the exercises used must be carried out in the proper mode of muscular work. Here we are talking not only about how long the work lasts, but also the duration of rest. In addition, after concluding each separate glycolytic training session, it is critical to complete several aerobic training sessions with the goal of clearing inflammation from the muscles. This can vary from two to six training sessions.

Table 7.9 – Several variations of the transfer process of developing sports form in middle distance runners where various types of competition exercises are used over the course of a two session training day model.

| Competition Exercises and their analogues being used | |
| --- | --- |
| First Session | Second Session |
| 800m sprints<br>600m sprints | 600m and 1000m runs<br>400m and 800m sprints |
| 400m sprints | 300m and 600m sprints |
| 1500m runs | 800m and 1200m runs |
| 1200m runs | 1000m and 1500m runs |
| 1000m runs | 600m and 1200m runs |

Transfer in the process of developing sports form is also quite critical for strength as well (Table 7.10), which by form of execution has many similarities. We observe this in local exercises (for example bench press and squat), as well as global exercises (such as snatch and clean). The transfer process of developing sports form appears in jumping exercises as well, carried out from a standing start (Table 7.11). These exercises are used in virtually all speed strength forms of track and field. The exercise with the highest degree of transfer is the repeat jumps for distance, as well as the five and three fold jumps from a standing start.

Table 7.10 – Several variations of the transfer process of developing sports form in cases where strength exercises are used in speed strength events of track and field. These are presented in a two training program variation. An athlete or coach would pick one of these.

| Competition Exercises and their analogues being used | |
|---|---|
| First Variation | Second Variation |
| Snatch | Clean |
| Clean | Snatch Pulls from floor |
| Clean pulls | Snatch |
| Snatch pulls | Clean pulls |
| Bench Press | Standing barbell press behind the head |
| Standing barbell press | Standing barbell press behind the head |
| Hang Clean/Jerk | Bench Press |
| Half squat (back squat) | Half squat (front squat) |
| BB back extensions | Half squat (front squat) |
| Squat (back) | Half Squat (front) |

Table 7.11 – Use of competition exercise or their analogues, used over the course of developing sports form using several jumping exercises in speed-strength events of track and field. These are presented in a three training program variation. An athlete or coach would pick one of these.

| Competition Exercises and their analogues being used | |
|---|---|
| First Variation | Second Variation |
| Standing broad jump | Standing triple jump |
| Standing broad jump | Jumping (extensive) |
| Vertical jump | Jumping (extensive) |
| Vertical jump | Standing broad jump |
| Jumping (extensive) | Vertical jump |
| Standing start five-fold jumps | Vertical jump |
| Standing start five-fold jumps | Broad Jump |
| Jumping (extensive) | Standing start five-fold jumps |
| Standing broad jump | Standing start five-fold jumps |
| Jumping (extensive) | Standing start five-fold jumps |

On the second level of programs we researched, the problem of transfer in developing sports form was examined when using three programs (Tables 7.12 – 7.17). It was planned that they would follow one after another. As they were planned, competition exercises and similar exercises were included. In those events of track and field where it is not possible to use these types of exercises, local or global exercises were used. This was generally applicable to middle distance runners, who used various jumping and strength exercises. The results achieved using this program, rotating these three combinations of lifts, are shown in Tables 7.12 – 7.17. The material presented in these tables shows that the transfer process from one training program to the others was quite high. Here the overall volume of training loads is critically important to the achievement of this transfer from one program to another. For example, if a group of athletes entered sports form overall in 48 sessions, then it took them 16 sessions in each program to reach that state of global sports form.

Table 7.12 – Use of competition exercises or their analogues, used over the course of developing sports form in sprinters. These are presented in a three training program variation. An athlete or coach would pick one of these.

| Competition Exercises and their analogues being used | | |
|---|---|---|
| First Variation | Second Variation | Third Variation |
| 60m sprint from blocks or standing | 60m hurdles from blocks or standing | 150m sprint from blocks or standing |
| 60m sprint from blocks or standing | 200m sprint from blocks or standing | 100m sprint or 110m hurdles from blocks |
| 60m hurdles from blocks or standing | 150m sprint from blocks or standing | 100m sprint or 110m hurdles from blocks |
| 100m sprint from blocks or standing | 60m hurdles from blocks or standing | 200m sprint from blocks or standing |
| 200m sprint from blocks or standing | 300m sprint from blocks or standing | 500m sprint from blocks or standing |
| 500m sprint from blocks or standing | 350m sprint from blocks or standing | 600m sprint from blocks or standing |

Table 7.13 – Use of competition exercises or their analogues, used over the course of developing sports form in jumpers. These are presented in a three training program variation. An athlete or coach would pick one of these.

| Competition Exercises and their analogues being used | | |
|---|---|---|
| First Variation | Second Variation | Third Variation |
| 60m sprint from blocks or standing | Broad jumps | 150m sprint from blocks or standing |
| 60m sprint from blocks or standing | Jumps (extensive) | Vertical jump |
| 60m hurdles from blocks or standing | Triple jump | 100m sprint from blocks or 110m hurdles |
| 100m sprint from blocks or standing | 60m hurdles from blocks or standing | Broad jump |
| Jumps (extensive) | 120m sprint from blocks or standing | Triple jump |
| Broad jump | Vertical jump | Jumps (extensive) |
| Pole vault | Jumps (extensive) | Vertical jump |

Table 7.14 – Use of competition exercise or their analogues, used over the course of developing sports form in throwers. These are presented in a three training program variation. An athlete or coach would pick one of these.

| Competition Exercises and their analogues being used | | |
|---|---|---|
| First Variation | Second Variation | Third Variation |
| Hammer throw and shot put 3kg | Hammer throw and shot put 2.7kg | Hammer throw and shot put 3.3kg |
| Hammer throw and shot put 4kg | Hammer throw and shot put 3.7kg | Hammer throw and shot put 4.4kg |
| Hammer throw and shot put 5kg | Hammer throw and shot put 4.5kg | Hammer throw and shot put 5.5kg |
| Hammer throw and shot put 6kg | Hammer throw and shot put 5.5kg | Hammer throw and shot put 6.5kg |
| Hammer throw and shot put 7.26kg | Hammer throw and shot put 6.6kg | Hammer throw and shot put 8kg |
| Hammer throw and shot put 8kg | Hammer throw and shot put 8.7kg | Hammer throw and shot put 7.3kg |
| Discus 2kg | Discus 1.8kg | Discus 2.3kg |
| Discus 1.5kg | Discus 1.2kg | Discus 1.7kg |
| Discus and javelin 1kg | Discus and javelin 0.8kg | Discus and javelin 1.2kg |
| Discus and javelin 0.8kg | Discus and javelin 0.6kg | Discus and javelin 1kg |

Table 7.15 – Several variations of the transfer process of developing sports form in cases where running exercises are used over middle distances. These are presented in a three training program variation. An athlete or coach would pick one of these.

| Competition Exercises and their analogues being used | | |
|---|---|---|
| First Variation | Second Variation | Third Variation |
| 600m sprint from blocks or standing | 350m sprint from blocks or standing | 1000m run from blocks or standing |
| 600m sprint from blocks or standing | 400m sprint from blocks or standing | 800m sprint from blocks or standing |
| 500m sprint from blocks or standing | 1200m sprint from blocks or standing | 800m sprint from blocks or standing |
| 600m sprint from blocks or standing | 1200m sprint from blocks or standing | 2000m sprint from blocks or standing |
| 800m sprint from blocks or standing | 1200m sprint from blocks or standing | 1000m sprint from blocks or standing |
| 2000m sprint from blocks or standing | 800m sprint from blocks or standing | 1200m sprint from blocks or standing |
| 400m sprint from blocks or standing | 800m sprint from blocks or standing | 600m sprint from blocks or standing |

Table 7.16 – Several variations of the transfer process of developing sports form in cases where strength exercises are used in speed strength events of track and field. These are presented in a three training program variation. An athlete or coach would pick one of these.

| Competition Exercises and their analogues being used | | |
|---|---|---|
| First Variation | Second Variation | Third Variation |
| Snatch | Cleans | Snatch pulls from the floor |
| Snatch | Clean pulls from the floor | Snatch pulls from the floor |
| Hang Clean | Snatch pulls from the floor | Snatch |
| Snatch pulls from the floor | Jerk from blocks | Power cleans |
| Hang Clean and Jerk | Cleans from blocks | Hang snatch |
| Hang Clean and Jerk | Clean pulls from blocks | Hang Snatch |
| Bench Press | Press From Behind the Head | Strict Press |
| Jerk from Blocks | Jerk from behind the head | Incline Bench Press |
| Inverted Row | Bench Press | Push Ups |

Table 7.17 – Several variations of the transfer process of developing sports form in cases where jumping exercises are used in speed strength events of track and field. These are presented in a three training program variation. An athlete or coach would pick one of these.

| Competition Exercises and their analogues being used | | |
|---|---|---|
| First Variation | Second Variation | Third Variation |
| Standing broad jump | Jumping (extensive) | Vertical jump |
| Vertical Jump | Standing triple jump | Five fold jumps from standing start |
| Standing triple jump | Vertical jump | Jumping (extensive) |
| Vertical jump | Standing triple jump | Jumping (extensive) |
| Standing triple jump | Jumping (extensive) | Five fold jumps from a standing start |
| Standing broad jumps | Standing triple jumps | Jumping (extensive) |

Translators Note – Extensive is synonymous with submaximal effort and intensive is synonymous with maximal effort.

## Transfer of Training in Special Development Exercises Training Twice Per Day

The mechanism for developing a state of sports form using similar exercises by form and function over the course of concurrent training programs is different for two session per day training as compared to single session per day training. This is explained by the fact that when using two training sessions per day, each second training session begins on top of the accumulated fatigue of the first. This leaves a unique door open for influencing the effects of transfer from one session to another. In our case, we are talking about the connection between similar and only slightly functionally different systems, which in one way or another influence each other in obtaining sports form. This is referring specifically to each individual exercise and its technical execution in either the first or second (specifically) session of training; Specifically, the way that being fresh or fatigued affects the nervous system and it's coordination of the movement. This has an effect on building transfer between the exercises of the two sessions by the way they are placed in the series of two-per-day training. During the first stage of training, athletes using the first and second training sessions used the same program for both. They did not change for the whole period of the program. The second stage of the training differed from the first in that the athletes used two different complexes of exercises that were different but only slightly, using exercises similar in form and function. This is specifically referring to the competition exercises and their direct analogues; in several cases it also included strength and jumping exercises.

The data obtained from the end of the first stage of the experimental training period demonstrates that over the course of the first and second training sessions, when using the same competition exercises or their analogues as well as local and global accessory exercises (strength or jumping), show that there was no difference between one session per day and two per day training in terms of sports results. This can only mean that the nerve centers of the brain are fatigued after the first session and the process of transfer is inhibited in the second session. Also, the athletes who trained twice per day entered sports form in half the time (number of days) as compared to the once per day athletes.

Moving on to the second stage of the training experiment, where athletes used two different programs that contained exercises slightly different in form and function from one another, there were some interesting findings between the morning and afternoon training sessions. The second program (afternoon session) was specifically designed to use those centers of the nervous system that were highly active in the morning session, just in different exercises. What this means is that there is passive activation of the remaining potentiation in those nerve centers. We call it "passive" activation because the given mechanical execution (specific exercise) is different than the morning session, but in terms of overall contribution by the nervous system, it is the same.

We called this effect "the phenomenon of passive activation." As a result of this finding, we discovered that a second activation of the complex of nervous centers exists, which take an active part in the process of carrying out the first program.

Here, as a result of repeated passive activation of the remaining nerve potentiation in certain systems of the body, the process of building long-term adaptations is prolonged, at the end of which the athlete enters the state of sporting form. Because of this, it follows that the athlete will enter into sports form in exercises used during the first program and in the second. With all of this in mind, we can make the assertion that the process of entering into sports form in the first complex of exercises will occur in half the time, based on the of number of training sessions. As in the first case, the same is true of the second, where athletes must carry out the same number of set training sessions (specific to each individual), to enter into sports form.  For example, 48 sessions. From this example, if an athlete trains six sessions per week using the first program (AM) after 4 weeks of training and the second program (PM) – 8 weeks of training, sports form will be achieved.

Figure 7.1 shows the mechanics of achieving this phenomenon of passive activation in training hammer throwers, who used (in the AM training session) a 7.26kg implement and (in the PM session) a 9kg hammer. We would like to note that over the course of morning and afternoon training, the athletes used a varied complex of strength (5) and throwing (one) exercises. Now, in classical physiology it is set forth that each exercise has a highly specific and individual corresponding set of neurons within the cerebral cortex. Due to this fact, we will now go over a few of these functional systems as they relate to our pedagogical purposes here. At the beginning of this principle, we find the teachings of P.K. Anohin, which are called the "theory of functional systems." This teaches not only the process of formation of the functional systems, but also their interconnection and inter-cooperation relative to achieving various ends.

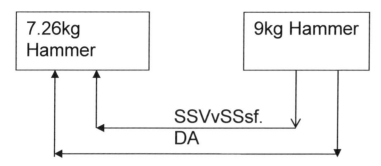

Fig. 7.1 – Schematic of the phenomenon of "passive activation" using two training sessions in a day. Key: FS – 7.260kg: functional system of hammer throw w/7.260kg implement. FS – 9 kg: functional system of hammer throw w/9kg. implement. SSVvSSf – Muscle action entering a state of sports form. DA: additional activation

This schematic of passive activation of functional systems in the hammer throw was observed using two complexes of training loads. This means that the second complex of training loads begins immediately when the first finishes, without a washout period. In the process of this experimental study, we are interested in the connection between separate training sessions in one day with not two programs, but three. The first program is comprised of two parts – over the course of the first the athlete, for example, throws a 6kg hammer; the second – carries out a complex of strength exercises; the third (evening) – this program differs in that it is comprised of a jump portion and a strength portion. In the first and third programs, the athlete uses two different implement weights. Over the course of the second program the athlete carries out various strength exercises, which stimulate passive activation. Here, the functional systems of throwing the 6kg hammer are activated twice (from throwing both of the weighted implements) and the functional systems of the 7.26kg hammer are only activated, passively, once (9kg throw). Eventually, over the course of one training session per day, the functional systems of throwing the 6kg hammer are activated 3 times (once active and two passive). It follows that over the course of one training day, the athlete activates the systems for the 6kg hammer three times, the 7.26kg twice, and the 9kg, only once.  Here it becomes clear that the calendar duration for entering into sports form in each of these functional systems will be different for each. The mechanisms for the action of passive activation using this structure of training, using a three-part training day, is shown in Figure 7.2.

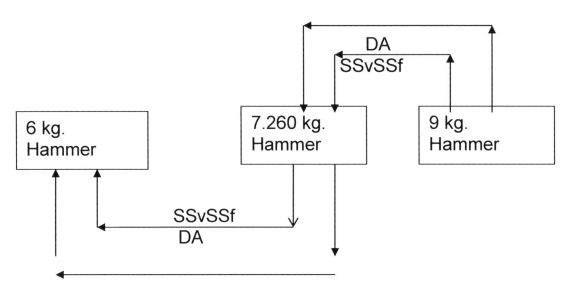

Fig. 7.2 – Diagram of the outline of "passive activation" using a three-part training program in one day.

Key: FS 6kg. – Functional system of the 6kg hammer throw
       SSvSSf – Speed of entry into sports form
       DA – Additional activation

Figure 7.2 explains the mechanisms of passive activation in secondary speed-strength events of track and field, as well as in several other strength and power exercises. In addition, in the strength of various topics, we never explored the experimental path of the given problem. Here, it is possible only to hypothesize about their existence. Without doubt they exist, but they have their own nuances. My explanation is found in Tables 7.18-7.21. Tables 7.22-7.27

show the mechanisms of the transfer process of developing sports form using two training session per day. Here, over the course of one training day, the athlete completes two sessions; thus, entering sports form faster than if they were only training once per day.

Table 7.18 – Combination of single training sessions, in a two session per day program, intended use of various types of running exercises, comprised of mechanisms of passive activation in groups of sprints.

| Exercises used in the first and second training sessions | |
|---|---|
| Session 1 | Session 2 |
| 60m sprint from blocks or standing start | 60m hurdles from blocks or standing start |
| 150m sprint from blocks or standing start | 100m sprint and 110m hurdles from blocks or standing start |
| 100m sprint or 110m hurdles from blocks or standing start | 100m sprint from blocks or standing start |
| 60m hurdles from blocks or standing start | 60m sprint from blocks or standing start |
| 60m sprint from blocks or standing start | Jumps (extensive) 30-50m |
| 100m sprint or 110m hurdles from blocks or standing start | Jumps (extensive) 30-50m |
| 100m sprint from blocks or standing start | Jumps (extensive) 30-50m |
| Jumps (extensive) 30-50m | 30-60m sprint from blocks or standing start |

Table 7.19 – Combination of single training sessions, in a two session per-day program, use of various types of exercises, comprised of mechanisms of passive activation in groups of sprints.

| Exercises used in the first and second training sessions | |
|---|---|
| Session 1 | Session 2 |
| Jumps (extensive) 50m | 60m hurdles from blocks or standing start |
| Broad jumps in series, Vault, or Triple (depending on event) | 100m sprint or 110m hurdles from blocks or standing start |
| Vertical Jumps | Jumps (extensive) 30-60m |
| Broad jumps in series, Vault, or Triple (depending on event) | Jumps (extensive) 30-50m |
| Jumps (extensive) 50m | Broad jumps in series, Vault, or Triple (depending on event) |

Table 7.20 – Combination of single training sessions, in a two session per-day program, use of various types of strength exercises, comprised of mechanisms of passive activation.

| Exercises used in the first and second training sessions | |
| --- | --- |
| Session 1 | Session 2 |
| Any type of squat (front or back) | Classic snatch or clean and jerk |
| Any type of bench press or triceps work/dips | Classic snatch |
| Classic clean and jerk | Any type of snatch pull |
| Classic snatch | Any type of clean pull |
| Clean or snatch | Shot throw 16-32 kg forward, up, or backward |
| Squat (back or front) | Good Mornings |

Table 7.21 – Combination of single training sessions, in a two session per-day program, use of various types of jumping exercises, comprised of mechanisms of passive activation.

| Exercises used in the first and second training sessions | |
|---|---|
| Session 1 | Session 2 |
| Any type of jump from a standing start (broad, vertical, or triple) | Jumps (extensive) 30 – 50m |
| Any type of jump from a standing start (broad, vertical, or triple) | Any type of half squat either front or back |
| Any type of jump from a standing start (broad, vertical, or triple) | 60m sprint, 60m hurdles from blocks or standing start |
| Any type of jump from a standing start (broad, vertical, or triple) | 100m sprint or 110m hurdles from blocks or standing start |
| Any type of jump from a standing start (broad, vertical, or triple) | Broad jump, pole vault, or triple jump with full approach |

Table 7.22 – Combination of single training sessions, in a two session per-day program, using competition exercises or their analogues in developing sports form in groups of sprinters.

| Exercises used in the first and second training sessions | |
|---|---|
| Session 1 | Session 2 |
| 60m sprint from standing start | 60m sprint from blocks |
| 150m sprint from standing start | 150m sprint from blocks |
| 200m sprint from standing start | 200m sprint from blocks |
| 60m hurdles from standing start | 60m hurdles from blocks |
| 500m sprint from standing start | 500m sprint from blocks |
| 100m sprint from standing start | 110m hurdles from blocks |
| 100m sprint standing start | 100m sprint from blocks |
| 300m sprint from standing start | 300m sprint from blocks |

Table 7.23 – Using competition exercises or their analogues in developing sports form in groups of sprinters. One jump will transfer to other jumps

| Broad Jump | Vertical Jump |
|---|---|
| Vertical Jump | Broad Jump |
| Pole Vault | Jumps (extensive) |
| Jumps (extensive) | Pole Vault |
| Triple Jump | Broad Jump |

Table 7.24 – Use of competition exercises or their analogues used together in the process of developing sports form in groups of throwers (shot and hammer).

| Competition exercises or their analogues being used | |
|---|---|
| Session 1 | Session 2 |
| Hammer throws and shot put 3kg | Hammer throws and shot put 4kg |
| Hammer throws and shot put 4kg | Hammer throws and shot put 3kg |
| Hammer throws and shot put 5kg | Hammer throws and shot put 6kg |
| Hammer throws and shot put 6kg | Hammer throws and shot put 5kg |
| Hammer throws and shot put 7.26kg | Hammer throws and shot put 8kg |
| Hammer throws and shot put 8kg | Hammer throws and shot put 7.26kg |
| Hammer throws and shot put 9kg | Hammer throws and shot put 10kg |
| Hammer throws and shot put 10kg | Hammer throws and shot put 9kg |

Table 7.25 – Competition exercises and their analogues, which are used together to build transfer in the process of developing sports form in groups of throwers (disc and javelin).

| Competition exercises or their analogues being used | |
|---|---|
| Discus Throw 2.5 kg | Discus Throw 2.25 kg |
| Discus Throw 2.25 kg | Discus Throw 2.5 kg |
| Discus Throw 2 kg | Discus Throw 2 kg |
| Discus Throw 1.75 kg | Discus Throw 1.75 kg |
| Discus Throw 1.5 kg | Discus Throw 1.75kg |
| Discus Throw 1.25 kg | Discus Throw 1kg |
| Discus Throw and javelin 1 kg | Discus Throw 1.25 kg |
| Discus Throw and javelin 0.8 kg | Discus Throw 0.6 kg |
| Discus Throw 0.6 kg | Discus Throw 0.8 kg |
| Discus Throw 0.5 kg | Discus Throw 0.4 kg |
| Discus Throw 0.4 kg | Discus Throw 0.5 kg |

Table 7.26 – Several developmental exercises and their analogues in speed strength events of track and field. These are presented in a two training program variation. An athlete or coach would pick one of these.

| Competition exercises or their analogues being used | |
| --- | --- |
| First Variation | Second Variation |
| Cleans | Snatch |
| Snatch pull | Clean Pulls |
| Clean Pulls | Snatch Pulls |
| Snatch | Clean |
| Standing BB Press | Incline Bench Press |
| Incline Bench Press | Standing BB Press |
| Standing BB Press behind the head | Jerks From Chest |
| Jerk from chest | Standing BB Press behind the head |
| Half squat (back) | Half squat (front) |
| Half squat (front) | Half squat (back) |

Table 7.27 – Several variations of the transfer process for developing sports form in cases where various jumping exercises are used in speed strength events of track and field. For use in a two-session training day.

| Competition exercises or their analogues being used | |
| --- | --- |
| Session 1 | Session 2 |
| Standing broad jump | Jumps (extensive) |
| Jumps (extensive) | Standing broad Jump |
| Standing three fold broad jump | Vertical Jump |
| Vertical jump | Standing three fold jump |
| Jumps (extensive) | Standing five fold jumps |

## Transfer of Training in Special Development Exercises

This challenge takes place in two stages. Over the first stage, in the time it takes to develop sports form, two training programs with different structural components are used. The first program uses competition and similar exercises, the second uses various complexes of strength, jumping, or other exercises. For each group of track and field events these will be different. For example, sprinters and hurdlers will use strength and jumping exercises where jumpers will use strength, throwing, and running exercises, throwers will use strength, jumping, and running exercises, and middle distance runners will use strength and throwing exercises. Similar exercises will be selected based on the fact that all the joints of the body are used. There will be roughly 5-7 exercises for 2-3 sets. The number of repetitions will depend on the intensity used in each exercise. For example, lets look at the complex of exercises over the period of developing sports form in hammer throwers. Using the "throws" program, athletes will use 30 throws of different implements and for their strength exercises, they will use: snatch, half squat, jerks, and leg raise lying on the floor.

At the conclusion of this training experiment, using two periods of developing sports form in different, by form and function, training programs, which followed one another, there was no observed transfer of training in developing sports form. In each of the programs, the athletes carried out similar volumes of training (roughly 48 sessions) to enter sports from. Analogous data was obtained using two-session training days. Over the course of the first of these, using competition exercises and their analogues, and the second, using a complex of strength, jumping, throwing, or running exercises. In this case, athletes entered sports form in an individual number of training sessions in each program.

# Conclusion

This book has covered in great detail several new aspects in the theory and practice of transfer of training. In previous manuals in this series, a great deal of time has been spent in evolutions of transfer of training itself. This volume covers in explicit detail new discoveries in the transfer process, which can be used to great advantage by practitioners in the field of physical preparation. I would encourage any professionals reading this book, who have not read parts I and II to go back and read what is contained therein. A great deal of useful knowledge and background to the contents of this manual are written there.

The transfer process is particularly useful for coaches of speed strength sports and events of track and field. Using the principles of the process of transfer of developing sports form and passive activation are of particular usefulness to you. In conclusion, I would encourage any of you who have un-answered questions about this or any of my books to reach out to me via my publisher. I am more than happy to expand upon the principles contained in this book and in my other publications.

31181515R00115

Made in the USA
Middletown, DE
30 December 2018